Additional material has been added to the English edition including but not limited to all but six of the color plates.

Translated by U. Erich Friese.

Endpages by Harry V. Lacey of breeding budgie with her hatchlings and egg.
Cover by Harry V. Lacey.

ISBN 0-87666-899-6

Distributed in the U.S. by T.F.H. Publications, Inc., 211 West Sylvania Avenue, PO Box 427, Neptune, NJ 07753; in England by T.F.H. (Gt. Britain) Ltd., 13 Nutley Lane, Reigate, Surrey; in Canada to the pet trade by Rolf C. Hagen Ltd., 3225 Sartelon Street, Montreal 382, Quebec; in Canada to the book trade by H & L Pet Supplies, Inc., 27 Kingston Crescent, Kitchener, Ontario N28 2T6; in Southeast Asia by Y.W. Ong, 9 Lorong 36 Geylang, Singapore 14; in Australia and the South Pacific by Pet Imports Pty. Ltd., P.O. Box 149, Brookvale 2100, N.S.W. Australia; in South Africa by Valid Agencies, P.O. Box 51901, Randburg 2125 South Africa. Published by T.F.H. Publications, Inc., Ltd., the British Crown Colony of Hong Kong.

ENCYCLOPEDIA OF
BUDGERIGARS

Georg A. Radtke

Contents

Introduction

About 200 years ago only the Australian aborigines knew *Melopsittacus undulatus*, the parakeet or budgerigar. In their language they called it *Bedgerigah*, which essentially meant "good to eat." These natives used to remove the naked nestlings from hollow logs and trees and fry them over an open fire. Incidentally, its native name eventually gave rise to the English name Budgerigar. Although in many places *Melopsittacus undulatus* is referred to as the "parakeet" (also spelled "parrakeet") in this book we'll refer to it principally as budgerigar or budgie to prevent confusion—because there are in reality many different "parakeet" species.

Nowadays this little parrot, with its wavy markings, is among the best known animals in the world, and it has become the most popular cage bird. It is not used as food any more by the Australian natives.

The greatest number of budgerigars live now as cage birds, and some which have been specially bred and trained give us much pleasure with their incredible sound mimicry. In addition, there is the show parakeet and its many color shades which entice the dedicated breeder to constantly try to produce additional varieties. The budgerigar is also a frequent research object in genetics.

This book attempts to gather as much practical information as possible for the budgie fancier and the serious breeder alike.

Georg A. Radtke

9

A wild, normal type of budgie photographed in flight. Photo by C.L.I.

Budgies in General

WILD BUDGERIGARS IN AUSTRALIA

This little parrot breeds throughout the Australian states of New South Wales and Victoria in the transition zone from open grassland to eucalyptus groves. In this area there is at least during the rainy season a regular water supply from small rivers and animal watering holes. The budgerigar is essentially a colony breeder, very similar to our crows, gray egrets and most seagulls. In these breeding colonies mated pairs will forego their own breeding territory and instead live in nests which are often separated by only a few inches. Such nesting density affords protection against enemies since many eyes and ears can detect an imminent danger far better than an alert but single male bird. However, the prerequisite for this is, of course, a highly specialized social behavior which enables rapid communication among individual birds through special behavior and particular sounds. Indeed, the budgerigar has a vast vocal repertoire and the ability for considerable mimicry, and it can react instantly. All these characteristics can still be seen in parakeets to this day, and it is these which make care and breeding of this bird so interesting, as well as providing certain challenges. Apart from minor arguments, most members in a budgie colony live together quite harmoniously. The females are somewhat more robust; in particular they have a stronger beak (as can be seen when a female which is not tame is picked up; such a small bird can produce a surprisingly painful bite). In fact, it is the female which chips away the soft wood inside eucalyptus trees to prepare the nesting site, provided a suitably

Newly hatched budgerigars.

large, decaying knot hole can be found in a tree trunk. Indeed, most parrots build nests in hollow logs and the budgerigar is no exception. Its eggs are pure white (they do not require protective coloration); there are usually four to six in one clutch deposited in a slight depression at the base of the hollow. Usually the female has placed some wood chips in this area or simply lays the eggs on top of the soft, decaying wood. During the breeding season the eggs are laid every day, and from the first egg on they are being incubated. The incubation period is eighteen days, and the young will hatch in two-day intervals, so that the youngest of five will be nine days younger than the one that hatched first. Therefore, the youngest bird is usually only half as large, because well-fed budgie youngsters grow rapidly. However, by and large the entire brood does quite well because the female takes very good care of even the smallest of its offspring.

During the first few days the nestlings will receive only a

protein-rich secretion which is produced by special glands in the fore-stomach of the female. This resembles the crop milk in pigeons; however, to be quite correct this has to be described as "fore-stomach milk" in budgerigars. According to TAYLOR, the fore-stomach of males does not contain these milk-producing glands. From the time the first nestling has hatched, the female will leave the nest only to defecate and for some short exercise flights. While the female guards and tends to the nestlings it is the male that provides the entire family with food. Even the female is fed by the male and thus receives pre-digested seeds, green food and probably also insects out of the crop of the male.

When the nestlings are a few days old even the male will participate directly in feeding the young. Once the youngsters have left the nest at the age of about four weeks, they continue to be fed for another fourteen days or so by the male until they are completely independent. In the meantime, the female will have most likely started another clutch of eggs.

At the age of eight days the nestlings can fully accept predigested food from their parents. At that time their plumage begins to grow. At first the whitish gray down feathers appear and then the primary feathers (wing and tail feathers); however, they later are protected by blood-filled sleeves for about three weeks. These sleeves eventually break open, dry up and shrivel and are eventually sloughed off; it is only then that the primary feathers are fully developed and functional. During this time interval the young parakeets look more like young hawks than parrots because the colored plumage develops very late. Once the young budgerigar leaves the nest it is fully capable of flying, and in appearance it closely resembles its parents. The only difference is the colors are not as bright and the tail is slightly shorter. The eyes of young budgies are jet black; the light iris ring of adult birds is still missing, and the eyes seem to be larger than those of adult birds.

A wild budgerigar photographed in Australia by L. Robinson.

Opposite:
A flock of wild budgerigars in
Australia being frightened away
from their drinking and bathing
area.

Once the young budgies have left the nest site they will never return. They tend to follow the male, begging for food, and thus they learn quickly to pick up seeds from grasses and from the ground in the open grasslands. Grass seeds are the primary food of budgerigars in Australia.

Flocks of young birds and non-breeding males take off in the early morning hours in search of food and return prior to the hot midday sun to the shade of tree tops. From there the males will tend to their family chores and remain with the growing nestlings during what is known as "social hours" (IMMELMANN). These peculiar "social hours" can also be observed among other small Australian parrots and certain finches. These small birds sitting in bodily contact side-by-side, and their green underside together with the black-yellow markings of the head and the back, blend in remarkably well with the green leaves of eucalyptus trees. This camouflage is further aided by the yellow sun reflections, producing a pattern of light and dark among the tree branches so that even such conspicuously colored birds as parakeets blend in remarkably well in the surrounding tree branches. In order to obtain drinking water the birds sometimes have to go on extended flights, depending upon the season and availability of water. The long, pointed wings together with the streamlined body make the budgie a swift and enduring flyer. Its flight pattern resembles that of swallows, and thus parakeets can fly over long distances in short periods of time. In the event it is pursued by a hawk—its main enemy—its swift flight and great maneuverability will often enable it to escape. In fact, budgies can obtain water in flight and even quickly bathe through shallow dives, and thus they avoid enemies lying in ambush at watering holes. When a water supply is not available the budgies can survive for prolonged periods of time by lapping up early morning dew drops on grasses, and they can bathe by rolling in moist grasses. Even this behavior can still be seen in domesticated budgies.

During the "social hours" the birds will preen each other's feathers (social plumage care). This behavior is independent of age and sex, and it is accompanied by the continuous emission of rasping and twittering sounds. Essentially, this tells them that there is no imminent danger for the birds and that they are in peace and harmony with their surroundings. Those birds which are tired tend to sleep safely at this time, pulling up one leg among their abdominal feathers and resting on the other one; invariably the head is bent backwards and hidden partially under the wing. Although some birds may sleep, there is a sufficient number of birds alert to detect any approaching enemy. A few short, piercing alarm whistles are sufficient for quieting the entire colony. A few seconds later an entire flock will take off in all directions. Once the danger is over the loud piercing calls of budgerigars—which sound very similar to those emitted by starlings—will gather the entire flock, including all young birds, together again.

Even during imminent danger at night budgies tend to scatter into all directions and into the wide open spaces around them, and, despite the absence of sight contact, they are always able to come together again. It is this behavior, as we shall see later on, that can cause the death of budgerigars kept in aviaries.

In terms of food availability and breeding behavior parakeets are very dependent upon the climatic conditions in Australia. It is very hot there during the month of December, while the coldest month is usually July. In the southern latitudes there may be occasional frost and in the mountains there is even snow. In central and northern Australia the "winter" consists of the rainy season, with daily substantial rainfalls and high humidity. It is at that time that the dried-out semi-arid regions awaken to a new life, which tends to activate the breeding instinct in parakeets. When the young have hatched, the first grass seeds will appear, which are the basic food item for these birds. As long as these grass seeds

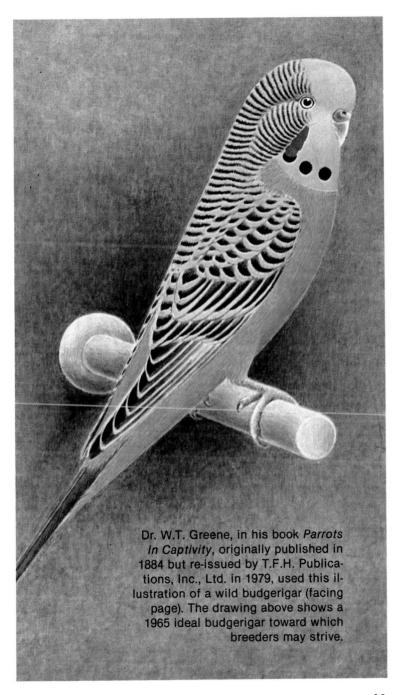

Dr. W.T. Greene, in his book *Parrots In Captivity*, originally published in 1884 but re-issued by T.F.H. Publications, Inc., Ltd. in 1979, used this illustration of a wild budgerigar (facing page). The drawing above shows a 1965 ideal budgerigar toward which breeders may strive.

19

are available, the birds will continue to breed until the progressive summer heat with its inevitable drought conditions causes the grasses to die and thus diminishes their food supply.

In our latitudes the breeding season of most species is dependent upon temperature and daylight hours. However, breeding among Australian birds is solely dependent upon the food supply. The temperature variations as well as the number of daylight hours are less variable in tropical countries. This is of fundamental importance for breeding Australian birds. Since the movement of parakeets is largely food-dependent, they can also be described as migratory birds; during periods of extended drought they often have to fly over long distances in search of food. In this search they appear to be guided by so far unexplained instincts which tend to lead them to areas which have newly emerging plant growth after prolonged droughts. It has been observed that in such areas of Australia's interior, parakeets suddenly reappear after an absence of several years. However, once the water and food supply has disappeared again, the birds will move on to other areas. It must be pointed out that these migrations, which often extend over many months, tend to take their toll, and only the strongest birds will survive. Periodically there will occur catastrophic drought conditions which last over years, and then thousands of parakeets and other birds will either die or become easy prey for predators such as birds of prey, snakes and humans. It is, therefore, essential for parakeets to be enormously fertile and prolific in good years, so that the species may be maintained.

Budgerigars grow to a length of about 15-20 cm, measured from the tip of the beak to the tip of the tail. The underside—that is, the lower neck down to the beginning of the tail—is bright green. The head, neck, back and the top of the wings have a blackish pattern against a yellow background with yellowish margins. The tail is long, with a step-like arrangement of feathers. The largest tail feathers are in the middle and of a dark blue coloration; the short outer feathers are bluish with a wide, yellowish cross band. The similarly step-like (growing) wing feathers, where the outer primary feathers are the largest, display an olive-gray color with yellowish green margins. The "face" ("mask") is bright yellow from top of the head to the throat. The sides of the neck are covered by longish, violet iridescent areas; these are interconnected through a small neck chain of six black spots.

The typical parrot beak is bent: the upper beak is conically pointed over the short, scoop-like lower beak. The tongue is, in relationship to the overall body size, rather large and thick. Adult birds have a yellowish beak; juvenile birds have a blackish one. Legs and feet are slate blue. The climbing toes are fleshy with a good blood supply, coupled with moderately long curved claws, two each pointing forward and backward. The nostrils are located on the top of the upper beak in a wax-like, featherless cere. In males this cere is bright blue; however, in fully grown females it is whitish blue to gray and sometimes of a deep coffee brown coloration. This clearly distinguishable sexual characteristic varies in intensity from bird to bird. Exhausted, molting or sick males have a far paler cere. In birds which are extremely ill or very old the cere becomes shriveled brown. Males in prime age and in excellent breeding condition have a smooth deep blue cere. In females this appearance is reversed; birds with a deep brown cere are the ones in excellent condition; old or sick females will have a chalk white to bluish cere. (This can be compared to the "male plumage" of older female birds.) In young budgerigars these distinguishing characteristics are not yet so well developed; however, young males can be recognized by their unblemished pink-violet cere and young females by their whitish-bluish cere. In young females there can be considerable variation; however, the nostril margins are always white. These characteristics can best be observed when the bird is picked up and looked at from above directly onto the head.

A double-eyed fig parrot isn't much larger than a budgerigar and is probably just as easy to breed and maintain, yet it hasn't achieved the popularity of the budgie (see a tame pair on the facing page) because present laws almost make it impossible to import them for breeding purposes. Photos by San Diego Zoo (above) and Walter Chandoah.

The surprising color variability of the now domesticated parakeet can already be detected in wild birds. Even some of the old reports indicate that among flocks of wild parakeets certain individuals were observed with yellow, dark green or even blue or opal colored plumage. Such unusual color varieties usually do not survive long in the wild, since they are more conspicuous and become easy prey for natural enemies. In addition, such color oddities encounter a degree of resistance during partner selection for mating, so that they are rarely able to reproduce.

BUDGERIGARS IN CAPTIVITY

When the British discoverer John Gould discovered the budgerigar in 1840 in the Australian outback, he was so fascinated with it that he collected a great many specimens and shipped them back to England. This gave rise to the desire to keep budgerigars live in captivity. Consequently, numerous collecting expeditions went to Australia in the following years to ship large quantities of live parakeets to the British Isles. Many of these birds died in transit and it is indeed surprising that any of them survived at all when one considers the lengthy sea voyages involved and the unfamiliarity with the ecology of these birds.

Eventually, ornithologists found out that parakeets, which in the wild feed mainly on grass seeds, will adapt quite well to millet seeds in captivity. They also began to be acclimated to the rough European climate.

However, it took quite some time—and then only through an accident—until scientists discovered that budgerigars breed in hollow logs. At first budgies were offered a wide variety of open nest facilities; the birds did not utilize these. The first female to lay eggs in captivity presumably did this on a cage bottom, where the bird made a little depression by tearing paper into small shreds. At that time it was customary to offer hollow coconuts into which a small side entrance was cut as nest facilities to finches. Since many hobbyists used to keep finches and budgerigars together—in large aviaries this was quite an acceptable arrangement—this then provided nest facilities to the parakeets too.

Thus, budgerigar females had to squeeze into the far too small hollow coconuts when the breeding season approached. Despite such inadequate arrangements the first parakeets were raised in captivity, a true sign for the incredible adaptability of these birds. For years thereafter the hollow coconut was considered the only suitable nest for budgerigars. Although the initial breeding success was not too overwhelming this was not too critical, since until the beginning of the 20th century large numbers of birds were imported directly from Australia. With time cage bird fanciers became more experienced in breeding these birds, thus reducing any losses and keeping prices down.

Eventually, budgerigars were also introduced into other European countries, particularly into France and Germany. The mild climate of southern France was most suitable for these birds; in the region of Toulouse large commercial hatchery operations developed. Therefore, the budgerigar trade became less dependent upon importers, which were virtually eliminated through protective measures by the Australian government in the 1920's. AF ENEHJELM reports that the first parakeets in Germany were bred successfully in Berlin in 1855.

Eventually, bird breeders realized that breeding successes among parakeets could be substantially increased if larger nest boxes were provided. At first one tried to provide hollow tree stems with the tree bark still intact; however, one soon realized that the adaptable budgerigar would just as readily accept artificial nest boxes, as long as these were sufficiently large and contained an even, shallow depression. Now all prerequisites for domestication were met and the parakeet became a true cage bird. Yet to this day one has to consider this small parrot a relatively young "pet" which has still retained all of its natural instincts. This fact has to be

Europe saw its first
budgies in 1840 when
John Gould sent some
to England. Photo by
C.L.I.

taken into account by those who keep and breed parakeets, since it has a profound effect on the successful husbandry of this bird. Domestication also includes external changes, something to which the budgie is very susceptible. Once the animal is under the care and protection of humans it does not need protective coloration, and it does not have to be as agile. Thus, fur and plumage colors soon become brighter and the animal itself becomes larger and slower. At first these changes are noted for further selective breeding. Because of its rapid growth and early maturation the parakeet is frequently used for experimental purposes, since it is highly adaptable and requires little specific care. The selective breeding of budgerigars has been expanded in two main directions. In Germany one was mainly concerned with changes in plumage colors and with determining the underlying genetic laws. In England, however, the breeders concentrated upon improving the harmonic body shapes and the overall size of the bird. Since the turn of the century the British have been particularly successful in producing valuable races of show and performance animals. One only has to remember race horses and dogs bred in England.

Consequently, in less than 150 years the parakeet has become a colorful house pet, a scientific research animal and a beautiful show bird. Shows and contests where the birds are judged by rigid standards are among the favorite activities of bird fanciers. A contributing factor to the popularity of budgerigars is the ease of taming them and their incredible capacity for mimicry of many sounds—including the human voice.

MAINTENANCE, CARE AND LONGEVITY

Before the turn of the century popular consent among aviculturists was that budgerigars could only be kept in individual pairs. Therefore, the French called them *inseparables,* a term which was later given to the African dwarf parrots of the genus *Agapornis* for similar considerations (the popular love birds). One thought that one partner of a mated pair would follow the other when one had died and that an individual bird could not be kept at all. There is some truth to this, because it takes a pair of these birds to show the total charm of this delightful parrot. Even more attractive is, of course, a small flock kept in an aviary. Since then it has also been shown that the artificial raising of abandoned nestlings is also quite possible and, therefore, individual parakeets do quite well and form a particularly close relationship with those who keep them. Thus, such a bird will become strongly imprinted upon humans, considering these to be its parents and later on their friend and companion. Nowadays we know that even a normally raised parakeet can become very tame if given the proper care and attention. In fact, birds up to an age of about six months can still be tamed; older ones do not take too kindly to being separated from other birds and do not become tame easily. Therefore, it is better to start out with a pair (or two males; two females kept together usually do not get along well with each other). In any event it is of paramount importance that one should always start out with young birds (for details about recognizing young birds, please see the details mentioned above). Legitimate dealers and breeders usually do not attempt to deceive their customers.

Apart from proper nutrition, the location of the cage and the room temperature are very important. Ideally, the cage should be at eye level. If it is positioned higher or lower the birds might feel threatened by the imposing height of the people around it. Their instincts tell them that an imminent danger comes always from above (birds of prey). If the cage is positioned too high, the bird does not have direct and close contact with the people. Also unfavorable for parakeets is either dry or smoky air and high room temperatures. The birds will react to this with an almost continuous molting and a reduced longevity. These conditions can be alleviated through repeated airing out, indoor plants and water dis-

Apart from proper nutrition, the location and size of the cage, opportunity to exercise (see facing page) and room temperature are important considerations for healthy budgerigars. The two birds shown above are far from ideal show types, but they are extremely healthy as their clear eyes and alert appearance indicate. Photos by C.L.I. and Horst Mueller.

pensers on radiators. Budgerigars, like all other birds, are very susceptible to drafts. In addition, the cage should not be exposed all day long to the sun. As beneficial as a regular exposure to solar radiation can be, it also can have a negative effect when not enough shade is provided.

Television is reported to have a very negative effect on all cage birds. No doubt certain exaggerations have been made in literature in recent years on this subject. In any event, a bird cage should never be in the immediate proximity or in direct radiation of a television set. Apparently it is not the light emitted from the set that makes the bird nervous but the high-pitched sounds which cannot be detected by the human ear. It is also disadvantageous to budgerigars and other cage birds to be kept in rooms with lights on for prolonged hours in the evening. This can easily be remedied by placing a shade cloth over the entire cage. The ideal condition for budgies is approximately twelve hours of light during summer as well as winter. On the other hand, the budgie has become such a domesticated animal that it will take "naps" during the day in unoccupied rooms and thus will be very lively in the evening when its owner returns. In such cases the "budgerigar day" can easily be extended a few hours, particularly during the winter months.

Budgerigars come from open semi-arid regions and, therefore, are not used to bathing. This is usually a "learned" behavior following the example set by other birds in the same cage/aviary when a bird bath is provided. Suitable substitutes for a bath may be wet lettuce leaves or wet grass, in which the young birds tend to roll themselves until their plumage is thoroughly wet. This is usually followed by fluffing up their feathers just like those birds that have been bathing in open water; they will take oil from their fat gland into their beak and apply this to each individual feather. Those hobbyists who have an outdoor aviary will notice that parakeets will almost always take a shower in any rain, as long as it is not too cold. Invariably

TROPICAL FISH HOBBYIST
Helping marine, freshwater, and herptile hobbyists for 42 years

Temperate Marine Fishes

The Paludarium: A New Challenge

Since 1952, *Tropical Fish Hobbyist* has been the source of accurate, up-to-the-minute, and fascinating information on every facet of the aquarium hobby. Join the more than 50,000 devoted readers world-wide who wouldn't miss a single issue.

Subscribe right now so you don't miss a single copy!

Return To:
Tropical Fish Hobbyist, P.O. Box 427, Neptune, NJ 07753-0427

YES! Please enter my subscription to *Tropical Fish Hobbyist.*
Payment for the length I've selected is enclosed. U.S. funds only.

CHECK ❑ 1 year-$30 ❑ 2 years-$55 ❑ 3 years-$75 ❑ 5 years-$120
ONE: 12 ISSUES 24 ISSUES 36 ISSUES 60 ISSUES

(Please allow 4-6 weeks for your subscription to start.) *Prices subject to change without notice*

❑ LIFETIME SUBSCRIPTION (max 30 Years) $495
❑ SAMPLE ISSUE $3.50
❑ GIFT SUBSCRIPTION. Please send a card announcing this gift. I would like the card to read: _____
❑ I don't want to subscribe right now, but I'd like to have one of your FREE catalogs listing books about pets. Please send catalog to:

SHIP TO:
Name _____
Street _____ Apt. No. _____
City _____ State _____ Zip _____
U.S. Funds Only. Canada add $11.00 per year; Foreign add $16.00 per year.
Charge my: ❑ VISA ❑ MASTER CHARGE ❑ PAYMENT ENCLOSED

Card Number _____ Expiration Date

Cardholder's Name (if different from "Ship to":)

Cardholder's Address (if different from "Ship to":)

Cardholder's Signature

the birds will fluff up their feathers so the water will penetrate all the way to the skin; the wings are usually raised so that water can also reach the sides of the body. Tame cage birds love to take a shower under a slow running water faucet once they have been shown how to do it. (To do this one carries the bird carefully under the faucet or attaches a suitable perch or similar device close to the running water.) Just before or during dusk the birds will not bathe because they are unable to dry their feathers, and thus they could catch cold. It is usually not necessary to trim the nails and the beak in normally healthy and active parakeets. The nails and beak are kept sufficiently down through the climbing and chewing activities. In old birds, which are not active enough, one often has to trim the nails with a pair of sharp scissors. To do that one holds each foot individually against a light source in order to recognize and thus avoid a blood vessel, which must not be damaged. It is, therefore, safer to leave the nails somewhat longer rather than to cut too close to the blood vessel. The curved nails have to be cut in the direction of their growth so that sharp edges are avoided.

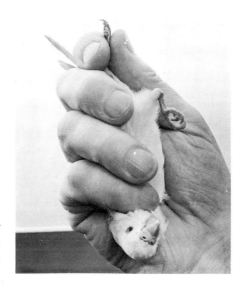

This is how to hold your pet budgie when you want to clip its claws.

This is even more important for the bent, triangular upper beak. If it has grown too long one should not simply cut the point off. In such a case one has to make a special effort to trim the beak along all three sides. Since the beak is rather strong, nail clippers are recommended.

Budgerigars can live up to fifteen years in favorable conditions. Breeding birds should only be used four to six years, females one or two years less than males. After that these birds enter a very critical period during which many of them succumb to diseases, including those tame birds which have not been bred. Once the seventh year has been reached a critical threshold seems to be overcome, and surviving budgerigars can then double their age and remain very active.

This is not a suitable cage for budgerigars since the wires are vertical instead of horizontal thus thwarting the budgie's natural climbing tendencies within the cage. But the ability to feed the budgie from outside the cage is satisfactory.

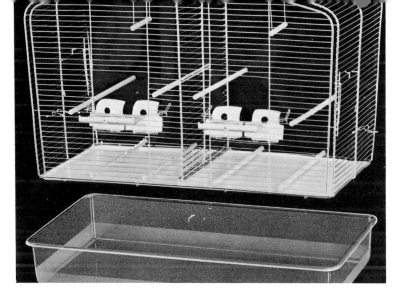

While this cage probably was designed with canaries in mind, the horizontal wiring makes it suitable for budgies, and the central divider and multiple doors offer considerable flexibility in use.

CAGES, AVIARIES, NEST BOXES
Cages

There are many different types of cages available. Some are made of metal, and some are made of plastic. Pet dealers generally can give sensible advice about which type of cage is best for your needs.

Cages for individual birds should have horizontal wiring so that the birds with the aid of their beak and feet can climb up and down. Such exercising is important for birds which have to spend their life in a relatively small cage. Also quite adequate is the commerical availability of perches and other exercise equipment. The more expensive cages have a suffi-ciently high plastic covering around the lower portion of the cage, which prevents the scattering of feathers and seed husks. Cage bird fanciers who have the time to use sand on the bottom of the cage can find commercially manufactured sandpaper. Birds kept in such cages can even pick up sand grains essential for digestion and are also quite useful for "grinding down" the claws. In general, most professionally run pet shops can provide proper guidance and advice. However, certain things have to be always kept in mind. First of all, a rectangular cage is preferred over any other shape, and it should be rather higher than wide. A removable roof, which enables the bird additional movement and particularly flight possibility is also quite acceptable. Budgerigars flying freely in a room will always return to the cage particularly when looking for food and, therefore, the roof can easily be closed once the bird has returned to the cage. Conforming to modern trends in furniture and household equipment, round, tower-like cages or even cages in the form of a pagoda are commercially available. Such an accommodation is only acceptable for a parakeet if it has the possibility to frequently leave the cage. Should such outside exercise possibility not be available for birds kept in such monstrosities, they have a tendency to show equilibrium disturbances. Similarly useless are food containers which have canopies over them and which are often used in these tower-like cages (so that the seeds will not become contaminated with bird droppings). It has been observed many times that young birds unfamiliar with such containers have died of starvation simply by not finding the food. Therefore, experienced breeders will never use such seed containers and instead prefer open containers or automated feeders. Most young birds are used to being able to see their food from above; when a covered food container is used they simply cannot find the food. Anybody who is determined to use such covered seed containers in conjunction with their tall cages should place the seeds on the cage bottom until it has been determined that the birds are actually finding the food inside the container.

Other potentially dangerous pieces of equipment for young and inexperienced birds are bells and mirrors which are suspended by a string or small chain and which are even standard equipment in commercially available cages. Young birds are prone to hang themselves or even break a leg when they become entangled with their banded legs. Many such birds have been lost in this manner. Any serious bird fancier will invariably avoid such "toys" in his cages. Invariably, birds will not miss these, particularly when they have never had the opportunity to become familiar with them. However, for a parakeet kept alone in a cage such toys might indeed contribute to its well being, particularly when it thinks it sees a companion when looking in a mirror or when it can play with a bell which seems to respond with sounds. In any event, such toys should only be introduced once the bird is somewhat older and more experienced.

Plastic feeding dispensers have proven to be very useful for seeds and water. It is important though that these devices be placed in such a position that the birds can reach them easily from their perches. Newly introduced birds should be closely watched until actually seen taking food and water from such dispensers. Until this has been definitely determined, additional food and water in open containers should be placed in the cage. It is only then the bird fancier can go on a short vacation, since the birds are amply supplied. Water in such dispensers remains fresh and clean for quite some time and the amount of seeds needed can also be predetermined, when one considers that a healthy parakeet requires about one heaping teaspoon or more of seeds per day.

BREEDING CAGES

The cage for a breeding pair should be at least 50 cm long, ideally even longer (60-80 cm); the height and depth are not so important. It is sufficient if such a cage is 30-40 cm high as well as deep and that the nest box is fastened to the outside of the cage (this is important for close supervision of nesting activities).

When only one or two pairs are to be bred it is even easier

to use an all metal cage, which not only looks good but is also easily cleaned. Such cages are also available with a removable partition, which can then provide two separate breeding facilities. This then avoids fighting amongst the birds.

A larger arrangement of breeding cages is used in the form of suitable sub-divisions within a larger structure. In this fashion one can then build several rows of cages along one wall. Such breeding cages are easily constructed out of wood or plastic whereby only the front consists of wire mesh, which is commercially available in different sizes. Each cage has a large access door for food and for catching birds in the lower third, and two additional doors in the upper third against which the nest boxes are attached. The inner partition, constructed out of a wire mesh inside a wooden frame, should be removable. In this manner one can provide large flight cages when the birds are not breeding. However, while breeding, the birds cannot disturb each other.

In professional breeding facilities, there is considerable variability in the type of cage floors used. Drawer-type removable trays made of metal or masonite and operating inside metal grooves above a wooden floor are very popular for individual cage units. Some breeders simply use large metal or plastic plates, covering an entire battery of breeding units, and easily exchangeable. This permits easy cleaning and reduces the danger of parasites. A hinged board to cover the gap between cage floor and front wire mesh prevents bird droppings and other debris from falling into the cages below. It also stops birds from escaping through this open space.

Breeders in the United States sometimes use all-metal cage units with wire-mesh bottoms. In such an arrangement the cages are elevated on sufficiently high supports so that the droppings, feathers and seed shells can fall onto the ground and can thus easily be removed. It is, therefore, essential, when such a breeding cage arrangement is used, that the breeding room or other facility have a smooth concrete floor.

This is an excellent budgerigar cage with a bottom in which water compartments and seed compartments have been molded. It even has splash guards to protect the furniture when the bird bathes.

Each breeding compartment must be equipped with a suspended feed dispenser and with additional containers for dietary supplements, all of them to be easily available to the birds. Absolutely essential for proper digestion and to meet all mineral requirements are, of course, containers for sand and shell grit, although parakeets usually prefer to pick this material off the ground. Such a breeding facility may well be highly efficient from an operational point of view and still not meet all of the requirements of parakeets, particularly since these birds like to "walk" on the ground. In addition, one has to remember that young birds newly out of their nest stay predominantly on the cage floor, where they can easily sustain an injury on the rough wire-mesh bottom or even catch cold from drafts. Therefore, modern technology is not always the best approach, particularly for breeders.

Fanciers on a modest budget can also substitute the commercially available mesh cage fronts with chicken wire. However, such wire has to be treated to prevent poisoning of the birds or their injury or escape. It is advisable to give the wire a protective coating of non-toxic black paint; the paint has to be *thoroughly* dry before the birds are introduced. In any event, the commercially available wire-mesh cage fronts are far more attractive and neater-looking.

Plastic coated aviary wire-mesh is unsuitable for parakeets; with their strong and nimble beaks these birds tend to remove the plastic material in a short period of time. Invariably, plastic bits and pieces are eaten by the birds, causing severe, often fatal digestive problems. Moreover, once the plastic coating has been removed the wire will quickly rust through.

Many useful hints and suggestions about how to build breeding boxes and aviaries are given in the T.F.H. Publication *Building An Aviary,* by Prof. Carl Naether & Dr. Matthew M. Vriends.

When the birds can be attended to daily—an essential aspect of successful bird husbandry—it is sufficient to use open, round or oval porcelain or earthenware containers for seeds and food supplements. Plastic containers are too light and are easily turned over by the birds. Drinking water should ideally be given, even in breeding cages, in automatic dispensers squeezed between adjacent vertical wires. It is usually sufficient to change the water every three days, as long as it does not get too warm (summer months) and unless more water is required for larger numbers of birds kept in the same cage. It must be pointed out that parakeets tend to drink more water when they have chicks; otherwise their water consumption is extraordinarily small. Automatic drinking water columns are particularly suitable for breeding cages, since water soluble additives (vitamins) will last especially long in such containers.

Also commercially available for breeding cages are seed dispensers with three holes. Some brands are better than others; sometimes a fancier with the right tools and a flair for design can build a feeder to suit his birds' particular needs. It is important that the seed flow remain uninterrupted and that the shell collector actually retain the empty shells. Otherwise, birds may starve to death in front of a full seed dispenser, or the seed tray may become blocked with empty shells so that the seeds cannot run freely. In any event,

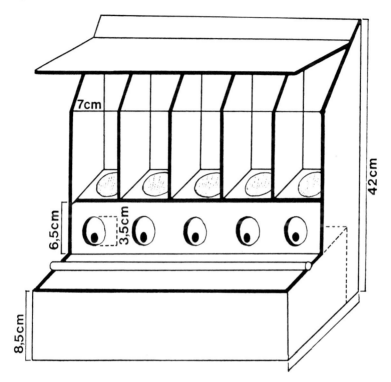

A proposed automatic bird seed dispenser discussed on page 49.

automatic feed dispensers must never be used for seeds covered with cod-liver oil or containing other oily supplements. Under these circumstances individual seed grains tend to stick together and block even the most efficient dispenser in a short period of time. Seeds coated with cod-liver oil must always be offered in a separate dish.

Shell grit can best be given in small, commercially available containers attached to the wire front or sides of the cage, where they are squeezed between adjacent wire strands close to a perch.

Commercially available perches are often too thin and too smooth, especially for the heavy breeding birds from the British race of budgerigars. Unable to get a good grip on thin perches, the birds become insecure and the fertility rate declines. Suitable perches must have a diameter of about 2.5 cm to 3 cm, and they need not necessarily be round. Nowadays, many professional breeders use rectangular perches with good success. Such perches can easily be made in any workshop.

Each breeding cage or compartment should have two perches. They should be sufficiently apart to force the birds to actually fly the distance (or at least lift their wings), but also far enough away from the cage walls so that birds do not damage their tail feathers.

Breeding rooms should ideally be bright, dry and well-ventilated, but they must not be so dry that the embryos die. Most suitable is a sky-light or ceiling-mounted artificial light source, so that the available illumination is evenly distributed throughout the room and reaches all cages and cage levels. Breeding cages should not be placed immediately adjacent to or directly under sky-lights. Basement rooms are only suitable if they meet the above prerequisites.

Birds require a large amount of oxygen, a requirement which has to be kept in mind at all times. Overcrowding of cages and aviaries must be avoided under all circumstances. While it is possible to "cover" all four walls with batteries of cages in a well-ventilated but draft-free room, additional cages must NEVER be placed in the middle of such a room. This arrangement not only makes servicing the cages more difficult, but it also affects the well-being of the birds by enabling the spread of diseases and thus ultimately reducing breeding results. An ideal situation is to place breeding cages only on the two longest walls in a rectangular room; the quarantine and holding cages, as well as other equipment food containers, can then be placed along the two shorter walls. Advanced British budgerigar breeders tend to arrange their breeding cages in a manner where there remains ample space along the outside of the cages. In this space thus provided they attach training (conditioning) cages into which the birds can move on their own through inter-connecting gates. Such an arrangement tends to facilitate an early conditioning of the birds to the show-cage environment. During this conditioning period all cage partitions are removed, so that all young birds are together in one large aviary-type enclosure. From there individual birds are selectively removed into the training cages by baiting them with spray millet or green feed. Initially the birds are kept only a short period of time in these new cages. However, gradually this period is increased until the birds can be left in there unattended for prolonged periods of time. This way the parakeets become conditioned to a "show environment" very early on. Usually old show cages are used as conditioning cages. This enables the breeder to present any bird to a potential customer in a show cage and thus demonstrate a particular bird's features (as per official show standards) under the proper conditions.

Nearly all German budgerigar breeders use sand on the bottom of their cages; river sand is most suitable for this purpose (in the proximity of the sea, beach sand is also quite useful because of the mineral content). Budgerigars, which are mainly seed eaters, will pick up small sand grains, which then act as "millstones" in their gizzards. Thus, seed grains are ground up in a preliminary step in the digestive process. This also tends eventually to wear down the sand grains, which are then passed out, so that the birds have to replace them constantly. Therefore, it is imperative that there always be a fresh sand supply available, particularly if coarse sawdust should be used on the cage bottom, a practice which is receiving increasing attention. Sawdust tends to bind the fluid waste products and thus keep the cage bottom dry. Some breeders even use peat moss in their cages. In any event, sand should then always be offered to the birds in a small separate container.

Budgerigars need not be kept in heated enclosures as long

as their environment remains frost-free. Although they can take the occasional frost in an outdoor aviary, a draft-free, rainproof and enclosed (indoor) room must be provided as sleeping quarters.

If budgerigars are to breed during the winter months, heating and illumination will have to be provided. There is an increasing tendency to do this, so that the young birds are in prime condition for the early show and exhibition dates. Commercial breeders, which have to supply tame, "talking" birds throughout the year, use heated and illuminated accommodations for their breeding birds. After all, the peak of the selling season is at Christmas. In centrally heated houses it is often quite easy to connect radiators in the breeding rooms to the central heating system. Usually small, low radiators are sufficient, since a temperature range from 10^0 to 14^0 C is adequate, in fact most desirable for parakeets.

During the winter months an illumination period of twelve hours (similar to the natural conditions in Australia) is recommended. Automatic time clocks can be used to turn lights on and off, and thermostats can be used to provide adjustments for a constant temperature.

Fluorescent light tubes provide an illumination closest to natural daylight, and under such light the coloration of the birds looks relatively natural. Rheostats should be used to gradually adjust light (for a ten minute period or so, prior to turning the light fully on and off). This enables females which happen to be outside their nest box to return to their nest so that eggs or nestlings are not endangered by becoming too cold or even freezing to death. During this "dusk" period, males and those young which have already left their nest usually congregate on the upper perches in preparation for a night's sleep. The use of such light-dimming devices avoids the danger of birds flying in the dark, something which parakeets unfortunately tend to do. Even the smallest unusual sound is upsetting. For example, an individual bird unable to find a sleeping space and crawling around in the dark or even flapping his wings can cause the entire cage population to go off in sheer panic. The mildest consequence of such panic during the night is obviously tired and nervous birds the next morning. However, more common under such conditions are serious injuries, even death through flying into unseen cage walls and other obstacles, and very much ruffled plumage. Only breeding (nesting) females will stay in their nest boxes during such panic. Unfortunately, very heavy birds tend to break their eggs or even trample their young to death when upset by panic conditions outside their nest boxes. The continuous, wailing warning cry, emitted by breeding females, while the other birds are in a panic, tends to keep these birds from calming down.

Therefore, a night light should always be left on, since even very low illumination will prevent night-time panic among the birds. Appliance stores carry these lights, which are manufactured for industrial use and which do not require much electricity. A rheostat can also be coupled with a time switch, which gradually turns down the illumination towards a very low light level or eventually turns the lights off altogether.

Electrical heaters should be avoided, since they require a large amount of electrical energy. However, in emergencies and for intermittent usage during periods of considerable cold, particularly during the winter months, such heaters are very handy. Small coal or oil stoves, used at one time extensively to heat outdoor aviaries during extended cold spells, are dangerous even in an emergency situation. First of all, there is always an open fire danger, and secondly such stoves can emit gases which are detrimental to the health of birds particularly susceptible to respiratory problems.

Aviaries

In the long run, breeding budgerigars on a large scale in cages is not very satisfactory. These birds require adequate flight space for their healthy development, particularly during the resting intervals between successive breeding periods. Therefore, outdoor aviaries, which afford ample room for flying and are under the beneficial influence of light, fresh air, sun and rain, have proven to be most effective. If an outdoor aviary is not available, similar arrangements should be made for birds kept indoors. Regardless of where budgies are being kept, the most critical parameter is the length of the cage, while height and width are only of secondary importance. Budgerigars prefer and indeed they should have the longest possible flight distance. A width of 1 m is not too bad, *provided* the flight length is 3 to 6 m or longer, if sufficient space is available. However, an aviary should never be lower than about 1.8 m, so that it can be serviced easily and birds can be caught without difficulty. In order for the birds efficiently to utilize the available flight space, perches in the upper third of the aviary should be few and be spaced as far apart as possible. Branches and other natural, frequently exchangeable perches should be used in the lower third of the aviary only. Budgerigars utilize these in a variety of ways; they like to climb among them and chew on the bark, which keeps their claws and beaks trimmed. In addition, bark from leafy trees (preferably fruit trees, willows, beech and birch trees) provides certain dietary supplements which are very beneficial to the birds.

As resting places for budgies and for the "social hours", it is advisable to provide a step-like arrangement of closely positioned perches (particularly in crowded aviaries). These perches should be under the aviary roof, or preferably in an adjacent enclosed room, where all the birds can sit together without disturbing each other.

The best and most durable material for constructing outdoor aviaries is iron, either in the form of iron (galvanized) pipes or frames. This material, however, is also the most expensive. All exposed iron (metal) parts should be coated with a good rust-proofing paint. Hardwood (eucalyptus, etc.) is also satisfactory, and it even looks more attractive in a landscaped garden; it too should receive a protective coating to stop it from prematurely rotting. Softwood should not be used, since budgies will chew it apart within a surprisingly short period of time, unless all corners have protective metal strips, which, of course, requires additional work and is more expensive.

Details about commercially available wire mesh types and sizes have previously been discussed. It is advisable to use a double layer of wire mesh on the roof of outdoor aviaries in order to protect the birds against cats and birds of prey.

Prefabricated aviary frames are also available made of metal and easily assembled and covered with rectangular wire mesh. However, some models are too weak for such potentially destructive birds as budgerigars.

Prior to constructing an outdoor aviary some consideration should be given to the substrate on which it is to be placed. Very attractive, as well as beneficial for the birds, is natural top soil. However, a concrete floor is more practical; it is easier to clean and maintain, and the spread of disease can be checked through easy disinfections.

In any event, the foundation of any outdoor aviary has to be at least 30 to 60 cm below ground level, so as to be rat and mouse proof. The higher the foundation above ground level—into which the pipe or other frame work is to be secured—the more useful (and valuable) the entire structure becomes. The minimum height above ground is 30 cm. The entire floor can consist of poured concrete, or a section of top soil can remain. The birds usually prefer natural soil to walk around in and to pick up various minerals. Moreover, naturally sprouting seeds, often found in soil, are a valuable food supplement. Therefore, the availability of soil in an aviary can be taken advantage of by occasionally spreading a couple of handfuls of seeds onto the ground; the moist soil will cause these to germinate within two to three days; budgerigars eagerly eat these sprouting seed grains. Their search for such seeds resembles closely their natural behavior, which can be further reinforced by sowing grass and lettuce seeds. However, one should not expect the emergence of a lush green carpet of seedlings. The sprouting seedlings will be eaten by the birds, which in nature find the largest portion of their food on the ground. It is similarly pointless to plant bushes and small trees in parakeet aviaries. The birds will denude them in the shortest period of time.

The ideal facility is a solidly built bird house constructed from brick or double timber or presswood walls, which are further insulated with glass wool or styrofoam. It can be located in a courtyard and garden or have adjacent outdoor aviaries. In such a location there is the least amount of noise disturbance to the birds and to the fancier alike. Furthermore, the danger of an ornithosis infection is vastly reduced. If a choice is possible, the entire structure should be so situated that the outdoor aviary section points toward the south or southeast. This enables the birds to get maximum sun exposure, and at the same time it provides protection against wet and cold winds. At least two outdoor aviaries should be included in such a facility, so that the birds can be separated into sexes during the non-breeding season and/or to effectively isolate diseased birds.

Outdoor aviaries should have an enclosed section in the form of an indoor flight cage. Both are separated from each other through a door or hatch consisting of a wooden or metallic frame holding a piece of wire glass. Such wire glass is essentially transluscent and thus it stops inexperienced birds from flying into it. At the same time it permits ample light into the indoor flight cage, even on days when the window has to be kept closed. Somewhere between window and roof a not-too-narrow flight hatch has to be placed in each aviary compartment. Budgerigars tend to use such hatches quite readily when the window is closed, and they provide additional ventilation. The indoor flight cage can be smaller than its adjacent outdoor aviary. However, both enclosures should ideally be of about the same size. Here it has to be

48

remembered that budgerigars like to remain indoors not only on wet, cold days but also in the midday heat during the summer months. The outdoor aviaries are used predominantly during the morning and late afternoon/early evening hours.

A bird house should have a service passage through its center, from where the indoor flight cages and, through the door-like window, the outdoor aviaries are serviced. The interior doorways should be kept fairly low. While it may be inconvenient to bend down, this is still better than having some of the swift-flying budgerigars escape. This point is of particular importance if the outdoor aviaries also have their own access doors from the outside of the bird house. If sufficient space and adequate funds are available, it is always advisable to install a double door arrangement via a short enclosed passageway as access to an outdoor aviary. Such an arrangement also makes the theft of birds more difficult.

In order to feed the birds one has to enter the interior flight cage first, and then remove a variety of food and water dispensers and other containers from the floor of the cage. Far more practical and efficient is a somewhat different system; one or more large dispensers are placed at an easily reachable height along the interior walls. Such dispensers must have enough access holes to accommodate a maximum number of birds at one time and must contain sufficient seeds for several days. Since the seed is being retained behind a sloping glass front, only a visual control is needed to determine the feed supply. It is important to keep these large dispensers clean and, therefore, they should not be located directly underneath perches. In addition, several food trays should be attached inside the enclosure, along the central service passage. These should be at a convenient height and accessible via a top-hinged hatch. Thus the birds can be supplied daily with fresh drinking water, germinating seeds and other food items, which must be replaced frequently without having to enter the aviary.

Above the service passage along the roof of the bird house sky-lights should be installed to provide additional illumination as well as ventilation.

Radiators can be placed along the short wall of the building, or low radiators can be installed directly inside the interior flight cages.

The previously discussed breeding and conditioning cages can be placed along the opposing wall with shelves for feed and accessories below. This way everything is in one room, and such a facility can be constructed for ten pairs as well as for 200, including all their offspring. In England, commercial budgerigar hatcheries of this type have been built large enough to accommodate 1,000 pairs and more.

Nest Boxes

Shape, size and materials used are factors which are of considerable importance for nest boxes. Basically, there are vertical and horizontal forms, both with certain advantages as well as disadvantages. The tall (vertical) form may well save space. However, it prevents an early departure of the nestlings, since it requires a fair amount of energy for these birds to reach the nest box opening, which is usually located in the upper third. This form also offers less horizontal area, and, therefore, there is a greater risk of damage or injury to eggs or young.

The actual nest in a horizontal nest box is at the far end, opposite the box opening, and so the adult birds do not "jump" directly onto the eggs when they enter the box. Instead, they have to walk up to the nest. In this wide nest box, the male can sit next to the female without disturbing it. However, there is one drawback; through constant revolving on the nest the female's tail will invariably become severely bent. In taller, vertical nest boxes the female will automatically raise her tail, leaning it against the wall, since there is insufficient space. At an age of about three weeks the oldest

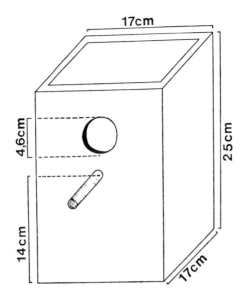

The illustration above shows a budgerigar nest box in the vertical format, while the nest box shown below is in the horizontal format. The circular opening in the horizontal mode is opposite the nesting site so the birds don't land on their eggs when they jump into the nest box.

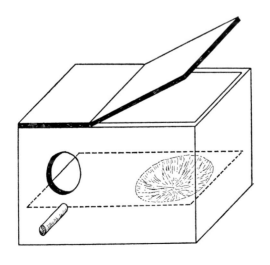

and most curious of the young nestlings tend to climb out of the nest and up along the wall of the lower horizontal boxes in order to look out from the entrance hole. From there some of them may fall out of the box before they can actually fly, or catch cold, or not receive sufficient food when the breeder is absent for some time.

One side of the *ideal* budgerigar nest box should be at least 17 cm, with a height of about 25 cm (the exact reverse in horizontal nest boxes). The entrance hole in both types of nest boxes must have a diameter of 4.5 cm. It does not matter if it is slightly larger, but it must never be smaller; otherwise older, fatter females—particularly those of the British race of budgerigars—may not be able to get through.

The actual nest should have an evenly shaped depression of about 12 cm diameter and a maximum depth of 2 cm. Particularly recommended are exchangeable, square breeding blocks with sufficiently carved out depressions, so that the eggs do not roll into corners or even out of the nest altogether. Most commercially available boxes are too small and too impractical, and so it is often easier to build nest boxes at home, according to available specifications. Nest boxes, with breeding blocks in the shape of removable drawers, have been most successful, since these permit close supervision of the eggs. Other types of boxes have hinged doors located in the lower third of the box, adjacent to the actual nest. In most boxes the roof can be removed for inspecting the nest.

I personally use vertical nest boxes which are suspended along the outside of the cage. Each box has a small hole in its bottom which fits directly over a wooden pin projecting from a board alongside the cage. The boxes are open at the top but covered with a hinged lid, which can be secured down by means of a hook and O-ring arrangement. This way I can attach either a nest box or a conditioning cage at this location, or I can keep the door closed. All this requires very little effort, and nest control during the breeding season becomes a routine matter. There are widely divergent views among breeders as to what is the best method; however, ultimately it is the breeding success which counts. The birds themselves could not care less. When they are really ready to breed they will do this nearly anywhere, provided some basic points are kept in mind, so breeding success is not impeded by inadequacies of the nesting facilities. This includes provisions for proper ventilation via small air holes in the upper third of the nest box; even a nest box lid, which leaves a small gap, is sufficient. However, if such an improperly fitting lid permits too much light to enter the box, parakeets may be reluctant to use it. If indeed a pair nests in such a box, the birds may appear restless, which may have a detrimental effect on the breeding success. The entrance hole, too, may permit some light into the box; however, too much will often keep birds from nesting. The same is true for nest boxes which are too dark.

Nest boxes should be positioned in the upper third of aviaries or cages, since many budgerigars like to walk on top of their nest box. Many professional breeders believe that females will breed more successfully when they can hear walking or "talking" on the roof of the box. On the other hand, it has to be stated also that other breeders simply place the nest boxes on the cage floor with equal success.

In my experience, a small landing perch placed just below the entrance hole is quite beneficial. Such a perch should be placed inside a drilled hole and should penetrate a few centimeters into the box interior. This is particularly important for the high, vertical nest boxes. This enables the birds to have an easier landing and entrance into the box. Later on, the male uses this perch for feeding the female and the nestlings without having to climb into the nest box and thus possibly damage the eggs or young. The protruding perch on the box interior also enables the female, particularly an older, heavier bird as well as growing youngsters, to reach the entrance hole more easily. Certain super-cautious breeders sometimes attach rough tree bark or some wire-mesh just below the hole on the inside of the nest box.

The most suitable material for nest boxes is hardwood, while the birds may prefer softwood, on which they can chew. Therefore, nest boxes made of softwood invariably last only a few short years. Similarly useful are nest boxes made of presswood (masonite), which have the advantage of being cheap. Plywood as a nest box building material is, however, not acceptable, since moisture tends to cause them to buckle and eventually split open, thus permitting parasites to enter the nest box. Plastic boxes may look good and even be very hygienic, yet they are too cold and too smooth and usually have inadequate ventilation. Moreover, there is always the inherent danger that plastic nest boxes may suddenly fall apart. I am not even aware of any cases where budgerigars have successfully bred in them.

On the other hand, quite practical and attractive in aviaries are plastic drinking and bathing containers, which can be secured into the ground. These containers have the added advantage that they can be cleaned simply and effectively. Especially in aviaries with mixed bird populations, where the other birds have greater needs for drinking and bathing facilities than parakeets have, these advantages are noticeable. Such containers are available commercially in different sizes and colors and are offered as bird baths. Even more attractive are bird baths constructed of bricks or concrete with a direct connection to a water main. In such a bath one can easily incorporate a water fountain, which is most welcomed by parakeets during the dry season and on hot summer days. A sudden "artificial rain" invariably stimulates the birds to extensive "showering" and even taking full baths. "Community bathing" of a flock of parakeets is indeed a delightful picture; on the more practical side it contributes to the well-being and attractiveness of their plumage and keeps the dust in the aviary down. The increased humidity also improves hatching results.

Feeding

NATURAL FOODS

Food determines the well-being, longevity and breeding success for all animals. In fact, the animal food industry for domestic and pet animals has developed artificial feeds which, as supplements to the natural food, contain all necessary nutritional components in quality. Many of these feeds even surpass the respective natural food. They are usually eagerly taken by most animals. Unfortunately, there are no such artificial foods for parakeets. As far as food is concerned, these birds are indeed distinctly conservative. There have been many attempts to produce an artificial diet for budgerigars. Well-known, large companies have tried, and for a while a pelletized food was indeed on the market. According to chemical analysis and appearance this food was acceptable to all—except to the parakeets. Therefore, we still have to rely on seeds from gramineous plants, *i.e.,* grass seeds, as the basic feed. Usually these are farinaceous seeds, which includes our various bread grains. Millet and canary seed are little more than cultivated grasses; these make up the "bread" for our budgies. Therefore, selectivity as far as the quality, country of origin and germinative ability of the available millet seeds is of paramount importance to all who keep budgerigars.

THE BASIC FOOD—GRASS SEEDS

Free-living budgerigars in Australia feed only for a relatively short period of time on fully ripened seeds. The rest of the year they take sprouting grasses, grass shoots, grass flowers and maturing seeds. This point is of fundamental importance in the biologically correct nutrition of budgies. Once a seed grain is fully ripened, it slowly begins to die, a biological process which can be hastened by a wet harvest or wrong storage. A healthy seed grain has its full germinating power—and thus remains viable—only as long as it remains on its stem. However, as soon as the grain is removed, even under the best of weather conditions, this grain begins to lose some of its nutritional value. Nowadays, modern machines can dry wet harvested grain with hot air, a process which accelerates the loss of nutritional value and germinating ability. Should this process affect the appearance of the grains, the seeds will be polished and chemically treated, procedures which are still used in many countries. The main agricultural regions for millet and canary seed are Africa, southern North America, South America, Australia and to a lesser degree the eastern Ukraine, southeast Asia and southern Europe (Spain and Italy). More recently, successful experimental crops of canary seed, which is less climate dependent, have been planted in Holland and England. However, the harvest from these two countries cannot meet the total demand, particularly since the crop size varies from year to year. The greater the distance these imported grains must travel, the longer the time from harvest to consumption, the poorer the quality. Unfortunately, there is little the budgerigar fancier can do about it, and even the grain imports often have to take whatever is available on the market in order to satisfy the enormous demand from cage bird fanciers.

Seed mixtures from reputable companies are usually of a sufficiently high quality. The breeder who buys his seeds wholesale should always test the merchandise for its germinating capabilities. For such a test one selects 100 grains and places these onto a moist, warm cloth. In moist, warm storage the seeds should begin to germinate within 24 to 36 hours. Germinating capability in excess of 50% is considered acceptable; far in excess of 50% is very good quality. Seeds with a germinating capability of less than 50% are considered inadequate and should be rejected.

Canary seeds and millet are fairly similar in terms of their protein content and other nutritional qualities. The British, who are world leaders in parakeet breeding, feed 80% or more canary seeds, and ambitious German breeders like to follow their lead. However, they tend to forget that the British have had a monopoly on the best canary seeds of the world, which come from Spain and Morocco. The rest of the bird fanciers have to be satisfied with canary seeds of lesser quality.

For our purposes a seed mixture containing 30% to 40% canary seeds is quite adequate. We then supplement this with millet. However, it seems to be indicative of the nutritional requirements of budgerigars that they rarely take more than 30% to 40% of canary seeds in a seed mixture. If more canary seed is given, this is usually left behind. The observant fancier will notice that most parakeets pick up millet and canary seeds in nearly equal proportions. Breeding pairs, kept in individual cages, often show periodic preferences; thus one pair may temporarily prefer canary seeds while another pair may like more millet. Yet, once nestlings are present the consumption of canary seeds increases, since these grains are softer and thus easier to shell. This holds true also for youngsters during their first few days after they have become weaned; at that time their beaks are still a bit weak and unskilled in shelling seeds.

Canary seed grains have an oval, elongated shape and look like miniature, polished barley grains. Millet, on the other hand, has essentially spherical grains of differential sizes and colors, according to the varieties available. Most suitable for budgerigars is silver millet, which has large silver-white grains. It is grown primarily in the United States. A good supplement for silver millet is La Plata millet, mostly from South America, although it is also grown in regions closer to

Europe. La Plata millet is relatively inexpensive and nutritionally quite acceptable. Since it is eagerly taken by parakeets it should be included in all seed mixtures.

The retail trade prefers the more expensive and far harder golden millet from Morocco (spherical, yellow-golden heavy grains); it looks more "attractive" in a seed mixture. The serious breeder, however, can do without it. Golden millet is relatively slow to germinate, and the hard seeds are—particularly for young birds—initially hard to "crack open". This is even more true for the red Dakota millet from the United States (heavy, rust-red grains). This millet is not particularly beneficial for the nutrition of parakeets, yet the trade continues to offer it for sale despite its high price. The inexperienced bird fancier often shops with his "eyes", rather than considering the nutritional requirements of his birds. On the other hand, the unattractively colored gray millet from Japan has a high nutritional value and also is eagerly eaten by the birds. This millet is only sold infrequently by a few highly specialized suppliers. Unfortunately, Japanese millet is relatively expensive since only small quantities are being imported. This millet strongly resembles miniature beech nuts, but the individual grains are much softer. It can also contain a fair amount of empty shells; however, this should not deter the serious breeder from buying this millet whenever it is available. It is indeed an excellent supplement for all seed mixtures.

The smallest available millets are mohair millet from India and the red and yellow Senegal millet from Africa. Since their grains are substantially smaller than those of other varieties, the birds need more time to shell them and thus they require longer to satisfy their appetite. Yet, these millets are nutritionally good for the birds and, therefore, they should always be included in the regular diet of budgerigars. It is advisable to use separate containers for these small millets, unless separate dispensers are used for all seeds—a commendable practice to avoid wastage. Senegal millet is not always completely clean. This usually does not present a problem as long as the germinating test is satisfactory.

Spray millet is essentially the same as Senegal millet left on the cob, often referred to as "thick cobs" because of their enormous size. The individual grains are clustered like grapes around the cob. Even when completely ripened, the grains tend to stick firmly to the stem. Therefore, spray millet can easily be shipped without the grains falling out. Although the bulky nature of this material increases the overall shipping costs and thus makes it more expensive for the consumer, the excellent nutritious value of this millet makes the price worthwhile. Budgerigars thoroughly enjoy picking on spray millet, and it is indeed a delightful sight to watch these colorful birds climb among the millet cobs suspended from the aviary or cage ceiling. The individual grains last longer in spray millet and they are thus a highly nutritious natural food product which is essential for growing nestlings and youngsters and for adult birds while breeding or during their molt. Spray millet is also strongly recommended for sick birds.

Most pet shops have spray millet packaged (three to four cobs each) as "treats" for tame budgies; most commercial breeders usually buy this millet by the basketful.

From among the larger-grained seeds, oat and wheat are quite acceptable for budgies. In fact, most pre-packaged mixed seeds contain about 3% to 5% shelled oats. However, it is more beneficial for the birds to buy unshelled oats directly and inexpensively from local farmers. Dried oats are particularly suitable as winter food in outdoor aviaries or for parakeets kept at low temperatures. Under these conditions oats are given as the main diet but are always offered in a separate dish. Once the birds are accustomed to this kind of seed they become quite adapted to removing the outer shell to get at the floury content of the grains. This procedure keeps the birds busy and their beaks trimmed. Moreover, oats contain vitamins and other nutritive materials directly beneath the outer grain shell, substances which are usually lost in machine-shelled oats. Therefore, at least a few unshelled oat grains fed regularly to the birds are indeed very beneficial. However, if too much of this is given during the warmer seasons of the year, the birds have a tendency to become too fat. This is particularly critical for parakeets of the British race.

Germinating oats are especially beneficial for growing nestlings. However, shelled oats do not germinate any more and will rot quickly when immersed in water. This is an important point to remember.

Apart from carbohydrates and proteins, oats contain vitamin E, which is essential for the production of eggs and sperm. Small-grained seed mixtures usually contain only very little of this vitamin.

Wheat, too, contains a relatively large amount of vitamin E, yet these grains, when too dried out, are too hard to be cracked open by most budgerigars. Therefore, only germinating wheat grains should be fed to these birds. Many breeders mix, with very good success, oats and wheat in a ratio of 2:1. Germinating seeds are of such fundamental importance for breeding budgies that this subject will be discussed again in greater detail.

OIL SEEDS—PROS AND CONS

Most commercially available seed mixtures rarely contain oil seeds. In fact, most breeders consider oil seeds as not important at all. Yet, since these seeds have a high protein content, a sparing use of them as a food supplement is recommended. Parakeets will take only food items they know. In order for them to become acquainted with oil seeds, small amounts should be added regularly to their seed mixture. Later on, oil seeds can be given in separate feed dispensers. In large aviaries there is little danger that the birds will overfeed on oil seeds. Parakeets are more moderate in their food intake than many other species.

Sunflower seeds and hemp seeds are suitable oil seeds, provided they are given in moderation. When parakeets are kept in a large aviary together with larger parrots (which MUST have these seeds) there is really no problem. As born imitators, parakeets will quickly learn from their larger cousins how the large seed kernels are to be opened. Since it will take them longer to open them—and thus they must expend more energy—the nutritional impact is effectively balanced by a larger energy consumption. If there are no other parrots in the aviary, hemp and sunflower seeds should be given ground up or at least partially squashed. However, such opened oil seeds easily become rancid and, therefore, only a daily supply should be placed in the cage.

Standard budgerigar seed mixtures should contain small amounts (2% to 5%) of niger seed, linseeds, poppy seeds and lettuce seeds. This order corresponds roughly to their respective nutritional value as well as to the preference shown by budgerigars for them. Niger seed is also very nutritious in the germinating stage. Some breeders also use germinating sunflower seeds; however, these are usually only taken when there is little or no green feed available.

Dried linseeds are supposed to improve the plumage (give added sheen) as well as aid in the digestion; however, germinating linseeds turn into a slimy substance which, of course, no bird eats.

Poppy seeds are very effective against diarrhea and, in any event, a small amount of these seeds will do no harm. Lettuce seeds are good but very light and rather expensive. When offered in a seed mixture, lettuce seeds are often "blown away" by passing breezes or by the wing action of landing birds. It is, therefore, more advisable to give lettuce seeds in separate dispensers or in small, deep dishes or similar containers.

Some breeders suggest that parakeets should be given

"wild bird seed mixtures." This is a rather uneconomical practice, since this kind of mixture contains large amounts of canary seeds, millet and oats, while the smaller and expensive weed seeds are often scattered about and remain uneaten. Besides, no budgie will ever eat the entire 10% to 30% rape seed contained in these mixtures. I strongly recommend that in an aviary situation all seeds be given in separate dispensers (or in dispensers with separate compartments). This should include as many millet varieties as possible and a substantial amount of high-quality canary seed (given in several compartments). Only one kind of oil seed need be offered, either niger seed, linseed, lettuce seeds or a little poppy seed, on an alternating basis. In addition (and depending upon time of year or season) a little dry or germinating oats, and possibly some squashed sunflower seeds or hemp seeds, can be given in separate, open containers.

For budgies kept in cages where automatic dispensers cannot be used, I recommend a seed mixture of 30% to 50% canary seeds, 40% to 50% millet (preferably in equal portions silver La Plata and Senegal millet), 5% niger seed and/or 5% linseed. Whole grain oats, given in a separate dish, are offered only during the resting period (between breeding cycles); in preparation for and during the breeding period, oats should be offered in the germinating stage only.

In preparation for the breeding season parakeets should receive germinating oats and wheat in the above-mentioned proportions. Other supplements have to be added depending upon the condition of the birds. If the birds are too fat, the ratio of canary seeds has to be reduced and oats are to be completely omitted; from among the millets, the silver millet may be omitted under such circumstances.

I usually give one cob of spray millet per day during the breeding season; sub-adult birds also receive spray millet (*i.e.*, one cob for every six to eight birds); healthy adults do not get any spray millet at all, although birds not in prime condition should be given ample amounts of this until their condition has been fully restored.

"Out of condition" refers to those birds which do not appear to be well or birds which are just recovering from a disease. This term may also be applied to birds which have just come back from an exhibition, an event which usually places a considerable stress on them, and to birds which are just going through their molt.

GREEN FOOD AND FRUIT

Fresh chickweed (*Stellaria media*) is the most popular and nutritionally the best green food for birds. In some areas, it is available throughout the year. It is partially frost-resistant, so that it can even be harvested from under a thick cover of snow. Chickweed often grows extensively on freshly cultivated farmlands, especially on light and wet top soils. Birds prefer this weed to have half-ripe seed pods, which are formed twice a year (spring and autumn). Apart from chickweed seeds, parakeets eagerly feed on the leaves and even on the stems of fresh chickweed. Since chickweed does not cause diarrhea it can be offered in larger quantities, in fact, as much as the birds can eat in a single day. Wilted, frozen or partially rotten chickweed is dangerous for birds and, therefore, it is imperative that only a daily supply be offered. In fact, this is true for all green foods given to birds.

From among the various lettuce varieties, parakeets tend to prefer lettuce heads. The dark, outer leaves are considered to be especially rich in vitamins. During the fall and winter months, parakeets will also accept escarole, but they are less fond of regular field lettuce. Spinach, green cabbage and mangel can also be used successfully when given in limited quantities. Another nutritionally useful green food, which is available during the spring months, consists of various young and tender grain shoots (oats, wheat, etc.), sprouting grasses and dandelions. These all promote prime breeding conditions and aid in the well being of growing chicks.

The only difficulty with all green foods is the fact that the birds have to become accustomed to them. Those parakeets which have never ever seen a green leaf certainly will not eat it; in fact, leaves blowing in the wind may even cause a panic among the birds in an aviary. Here patience is a distinct virtue. Fresh green food should be offered daily, even if this has to be removed wilted at the end of each day. In a somewhat crowded aviary the birds tend to go on to green food far more rapidly, since there is always one individual among them who has more "courage" than the rest of them, and it sets an example invariably followed by the other birds.

Green foods also include—in a larger sense—other weeds and grasses carrying seeds. The order of popularity of these among parakeets is roughly as follows: shepherd's purse, milk thistle, broad rib-grass and ragwort. Most of these plants are commonly found on filled-in garbage dumps, compost piles, and neglected garden and farm plots; the rib-grass occurs commonly along foot paths. Budgerigars will feed only on the *seeds* of these plants, preferably in a half-ripened stage. For the specific identification of these and other suitable green food plants it is advisable to consult one of the illustrated guide books.

Any half-ripened grass seeds found on paddocks, in fields and along drainage ditches are suitable as food. However, budgies tend to prefer risp grass, willow-herb grass and rye grass. These grasses are even taken by birds which have never seen them before; there are also many other grass varieties eagerly taken by budgerigars. It has been observed that escaped budgies would feed for weeks on various wild grass seeds and remain in excellent condition.

A prerequisite for birds to accept these grasses is, of course, the presence of actual seeds and the seed pods. Grasses which are still in bloom have, of course, not yet developed their seeds, so that they are of little use to the birds. Depending upon the grass species and the soil conditions, most grasses have half-ripened seeds from June to

September. The entire grass stems are cut off and then suspended, in bunches, inside the aviaries or cages; if need be the birds will also pick on them on the ground. Wilted bunches of grass should be removed daily.

Half-ripe oats and wheat shoots—usually available from June to August—are considered real "treats"; they are a highly nutritious growth food for young birds. The shoots are harvested together with at least half of their stem. This way they can either be suspended inside a cage or placed in a water container and thus kept for at least eight days in storage. However, it need not be pointed out that the respective farmer must be asked permission to remove some of these shoots from his property.

A potentially dangerous aspect of using grasses, etc. from gardens and agricultural areas in general is the wide-spread practice of using insecticides. An indiscriminate use of green food from areas treated with such chemicals has already wiped out entire bird populations. Therefore, one has to be absolutely positive that a particular area has not been treated. This also includes plant and tree nurseries, where one can usually find lush patches of chickweed. When permission to "harvest" chickweed is sought, one should inquire at the same time about the use of insecticide.

The potential danger of insecticide poisoning has discouraged many breeders from using green food altogether. Instead they prefer "home grown" foods, from germinating seeds to tender green shoots, grown in flower boxes and similar containers. However, creature comfort should not prevent us from attempting to obtain natural green food; it is invariably cheaper and nutritionally better for the birds.

Carrots and apples are good substitutes for green food during the winter months. In fact, during the breeding season, many breeders use finely ground-up carrots to moisten soft food mixtures, which are eagerly taken by budgerigars once they are used to it. Once again, it is a matter for the birds to become accustomed to such a food, something which is a bit

The yellow budgie has a good, open eye, while the blue budgie has a problem with its eye. This strain of budgies has defective eyes as their eyelids do not open perfectly round like the bird on the facing page. The light green budgie photograph is courtesy of Vogelpark Walsrode while the upper photo was taken by G. Ebben.

difficult since carrots are reddish. Most birds, and in particular the highly suspicious budgerigar, tend to distinctly mistrust this color. For budgies to get used to carrots, one should place daily a couple of carrot halves (sliced along their longest axis) squeezed between the cage or aviary wire, until such time when one bird finally starts pecking at it. This then seems to "break the ice", and once the birds have sampled the sweetish taste of carrot they will also accept ground-up carrots in soft food mixtures.

Juicy apples which are not too sour should be fastened whole to the cage or aviary wire, or cut in half and pierced onto a nail with a cut surface pointing upward. Budgies seem to prefer apples over all other available kinds of fruit. A similar procedure can be used for pears and oranges. Attempts with other fruit may also be successful. However, fruit should not be given in excess.

A bird fancier who owns a garden can easily sow risp grass and even spray millet with good success. Especially among risp grass varieties there are some which are largely weather-resistant. These, when planted sufficiently early, will provide large, half-ripened risps with thick, yellowish to reddish seeds from June to September. These seeds should not be permitted to ripen fully, otherwise their nutritional value will be lowered to that of dry, tropical millet. However, half-ripened millet is the best food; no other natural food available approximates its nutritional value.

Spray millet will not necessarily grow successfully every year; this plant is somewhat susceptible and requires a longer period to fully ripen. In some years it may happen that only very small cobs are being produced, with grains which may be hollow. Spray millet requires a protected plot with well-fertilized soil. The young seedlings have to be spaced out, if mature plants are to produce sizable cobs of spray millet. The seeds are usually not ready for feeding until September; if one waits till October sparrows will have eaten the seeds or they may have been spoiled by early night frost. Therefore, as a homegrown seed, risp grass is to be preferred.

MINERALS AND VITAMINS

Most of the previously mentioned foods contain these two vital nutritional components. Unfortunately, however, we can hardly offer our birds all those kinds of food they are accustomed to in the wild, especially not simultaneously and sometimes not even at the right time. In addition, bird fanciers in most industrialized countries have access only to commercially available lettuce as the only suitable green food (which must always be washed thoroughly before use).

Therefore, we have to be grateful to nutrition research for producing a variety of effective mineral and vitamin preparations. In this day and age, even sand cannot be used anymore without the risk of potential danger. However, pet shops now carry bird grit, which contains finely ground-up shell fragments and other calcium chips, as well as sand grains and small pebbles. Such grit is eagerly taken by parakeets; it aids the digestion, and its diverse mineral content promotes the growth of bones, and in females the production of egg shells, as well as supporting a good plumage in all birds. A mineral mixture must always be available to the birds, provided in a separate container. Cuttle fish are even more advantageous. Apart from supplying the needed minerals, they keep the budgerigar beak trimmed and at the same time provide a sort of occupational therapy. However, in rural areas many of the mineral requirements can be satisfied through available natural products. Clean river sand or beach sand (which must be changed frequently) is used to cover the cage bottom. A chunk of concrete is placed into the cage, and ground-up egg shells available from poultry farms supply the needed calcium.

Commercially available shell grit for breeding cages should be given in small containers suspended from the sides

Budgies are very easy birds to feed. While they enjoy millet sprays very much, they will chew on almost anything (see above) if they are given the opportunity, even if the plant is poisonous to them! So hang millet spray inside the cage (see facing page) and play it safe. Photos by Dr. Herbert R. Axelrod.

or the front. For use in aviaries, a large amount of shell grit can be placed inside a drinking water dispenser, so that it is not wasted or contaminated with dirt.

There are a multitude of liquid or solid vitamin preparations available, too many to be mentioned individually. All reputable products provide a complete analysis, either directly on the package or in an accompanying prospectus. Preference should be given to those preparations which contain the entire vitamin B complex, including the important vitamin B_{12}. Most commercially available seed mixtures are deficient in vitamin B. This vitamin complex promotes the metabolism and aids muscle tone; it is also essential for various nerve functions, thus a vitamin B deficiency can cause paralysis.

Liquid vitamin preparations are given—according to the instructions provided with each package—in the drinking water once or twice a week. This is particularly effective during the breeding season, because at that time parakeets take in more water than at any other period. At other times, vitamins can be given in a particularly preferred type of food, such as soft food, for instance. For that purpose one would prefer any of the various vitamin powders over liquids, since these can be mixed more easily into solid food. In order to assure that birds receive sufficient vitamins, this substance should be added in excess.

In the early days of budgerigar breeding, many breeders used cod-liver oil and some people still persist in using it today, since it contains ample amounts of vitamin A and D, which is particularly effective in preventing females from becoming egg bound. Other than that, cod-liver oil does not contain important vitamins, and old or spoiled (rancid) cod-liver oil is probably not very good for birds. Therefore, cod-liver oil should always be kept in tightly closed bottles and stored in cool places. It should only be used sparingly in conjunction with small, quickly used up amounts of food. Most suitable as a mixing medium is canary seed, where one uses—at the most—one tablespoon of cod-liver oil per 1 kg of seed (for a few birds, two drops of cod liver oil per table-spoon of canary seed). Such enriched food must always be given in a separate container, which has to be washed daily with hot water so as to remove all traces of old and rancid cod-liver oil. Cod-liver oil enriched foods must never be placed in seed dispensers, since individual seed grains tend to stick together and thus invariably block the food flow in such containers.

Budgerigar fanciers have to be warned against using any of the commercially available cod-liver concentrates, which are intended for use with larger domesticated animals only. These products are far too concentrated for cage birds, so that it is extremely difficult to measure a correct dosage.

If cod-liver oil is indeed used, the special emulsion prepa-rations for children are the most suitable. A cod-liver oil sup-plement is really only required during the winter months, or for use by breeders who do not possess outdoor aviaries. Those people for whom the commercially available products are too uneconomical might also find some use for it. Here it has to be remembered that cod-liver oil contains only a preliminary form of vitamin D, which is converted inside a bird's body into the final and effective form under the in-fluence of the sun. Vitamin C, which is so important in hu-man nutrition, is formed within the bird's body. Commer-cially available vitamin preparations—and there are some containing the entire spectrum of physiologically required trace elements—are only needed under the following condi-tions:

1) When it is attempted to breed during the winter months.

2) In large urban and industrial areas.

3) When birds are being kept exclusively indoors.

If birds are kept in rural areas, where they can be main-tained in outdoor aviaries and receive—according to the season—green food and/or fruit, and when the birds are bred only during the spring and summer months, then vitamin supplements are really not necessary.

9

10

11

12

13

14

EED GERMINATION requires any birdseed which is fresh. You also require (1)
n aluminum tray, a strainer, bowl, and plastic wrap. The strainer must fit into
ꞁe bowl and be able to support itself (2) on the rim. Fill the strainer with the
ꞁirdseed (3), and rinse it under running water until it is thoroughly clean (4).
llow it to soak for about a day (5) in the bowl. Change the water as frequently
s convenient, but at least once every 12 hours. Then pour the dampened seed
ꞁnto the tray (6) and spread the seed uniformly (7). Mix in any mold-inhibiting
ubstance (Moldex) and cover the seed to keep the moisture in, but not to stop
ꞁr from getting to the seed (8, 9). If you want to grow *grass* from the seed you
an use earth (10), sprinkle it with seed (11), mix the seed with the earth (12),
ꞁprinkle lightly with water (13) and store in a warm, dark place (14). The seed
sed with earth can either be soaked for a while (see above 1 through 5), or
ꞁtraight from the box.

Budgerigars are playful and intelligent. They need water for bathing and drinking. Imagine how you can use these facts to teach tricks! The illustration below shows a budgie taking special seed from a treat cup. Budgies love some seeds more than others, especially those coated with honey.

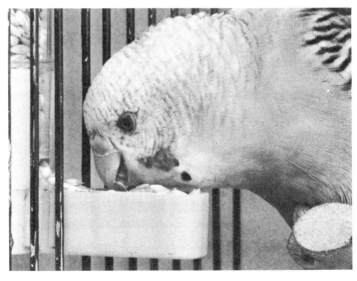

GERMINATING SEEDS AND SOFT FOODS
FOR RAISING NESTLINGS

If all other foods are unavailable, budgerigars will indeed raise their young on dry seeds alone. Unfortunately, a substantial penalty will invariably have to be paid for this in the form of weak youngsters, infertility, susceptibility to diseases, a reduced breeding period and shortened longevity.

The advantages of germinating seeds have already been discussed, and to prepare this kind of food is far easier than most bird fanciers imagine. Whole oat and wheat grains, mixed in a ratio of 2:1, are placed in a deep container and covered with water. The layer of grain should not be too thick, but it must be covered completely with water. If this layer is indeed too thick, an insufficient amount of oxygen penetrates through the grain layer, so that it may start to decay instead of germinating. The container is kept relatively warm about 12 to 24 hours. After about 12 hours the individual grains will have swollen to twice their normal size. Although not visible yet, the grains have already begun to germinate and a distinct physiological process has set in. Even at this early stage this water-soaked seed is already of considerable nutritional value. The grains are then thoroughly washed under running water until the water is clear, and they are then placed in a strainer to drip-dry. This kind of food should be moist—not wet—when fed.

Seeds which have been permitted to completely germinate are even more nutritious. In order to reach that stage, the water-soaked swollen grains are placed in a shallow bowl (without water), which is then covered with a sheet of glass and stored in a warm place for an additional twelve hours. The glass cover prevents dust from settling and it keeps the grains moist. After that time interval, oat grains will have begun to produce small white roots (all other suitable types of seeds will have the actual germ root growing initially at one end of each grain).

A very promising show quality young opaline light blue. The photo lights forced the closed eye. Even though this bird shows the typical small juvenile throat spots, it gives some indication of becoming a good type. The pure white head will emerge when the juvenile head markings disappear after the first molt. Photo by G. Tiedemann from the original German edition of this book.

The back view of the cinnamon opaline cobalt female illustrates the "royal" opaline, which has no markings on the shoulder and back. The color is a little paler than cinnamon violet. The other bird, also a female, is an opaline cobalt blue. Due to the absence of the cinnamon factor the coloration is more intense and it has a better head shape and mask. Photo by F. Siedel from the original German edition.

These well-germinating seeds are washed once more and then permitted to drip-dry again. Such seeds spoil easily and, therefore, one would only prepare as much as is needed in daily food rations. Parakeets will still remove the outer shell from germinated seeds, so that these remnants have to be removed and the container be thoroughly cleaned before it is used again.

In order to establish an effective production line for germinating seeds, three different containers are required; one is needed for the initial soaking process, the other for storing the germinating seeds and the last one for starting up the next batch. Once the logistics have been properly worked out, producing germinating seeds becomes an effortless exercise. Nowadays, a special three-part germinating apparatus, made of plastic, is commercially available. Its use is strongly recommended because of its simple operating procedure.

The various millets (silver, La Plata), canary seeds and niger seeds are also quite suitable for germination. It is often far easier to start with a mixture of these seeds; however, one has to keep in mind that the different seeds germinate at different rates. La Plata millet and niger seeds germinate within 24 hours (under favorable conditions), while canary seeds require up to 36 hours. This can, of course, be simplified by alternating the seeds used for the germination process, which then provides the parakeets with a more variable diet.

Those who also keep larger parrots can use germinating cultures of mixed seeds, containing oats, wheat, hemp and sunflower seeds. Parakeets tend to "sample" this food, which is also nutritious and highly beneficial for them. Yet, starting such cultures for parakeets only is uneconomical. Grass seeds are really sufficient for these birds, and if one wants to be especially good to them, the occasional lot of germinating niger seeds would be more than adequate.

With the aid of moist, germinated foods budgies can usually be enticed to eventually take the various floury foods used for raising chicks (usually such foods are quite beneficial for parakeets, but contrary to what is being advertised, they are initially not very fond of them). Even in the dry condition, *i.e.*, as it comes out of the package, this food is invariably rejected by parakeets. The birds show similar reactions to those foods which contain fatty additives to make the food "wet-crumbly" and which are advertised as being "ready to be fed." However, if this food is sprinkled over germinating seeds, the birds will invariably take some of the crumbs and thus become slowly accustomed to it. Eventually parakeets become fully used to it, and then they will also feed upon it when they have to feed their chicks. In order to raise an entire clutch of chicks on shelled, dry seeds alone, much less satisfy their appetites, the adult bird requires much time and energy to shell seeds and to pre-digest food in its crop. Here one has to remember that this same bird has been through much stress, by producing copious amounts of fore-stomach milk to feed the young during the first few days of their lives.

Moreover, dry seed grains have little nutritional value. The adult birds can fill their crops faster with more voluminous, and more nutritional, softer germinating seeds. These seeds are easier to pre-digest, since they do not require additional moisture, which otherwise would have to be obtained in the form of drinking water. Moreover, this sort of soft food can be more easily regurgitated and transferred to the nestlings.

All this is even more relevant when commercially available moist soft foods are being used. Once this kind of food is being taken readily by all the birds, it should always be offered in separate containers. Commercially available dry growth foods are being mixed alternately with ground carrots and apples to provide some moisture. This mixture must not be too wet, so that it sticks together in large clumps. Slightly moist-crumbly is the most suitable consistency.

Many breeders prepare their own soft foods, which requires more time but is also more economical. There are many recipes for this kind of food. One of the oldest soft

The world-famous Evelyn Theresa Miller whose budgie books date back to the early 1950's, bred budgies (or parakeets as they were called then) for their friendliness and charm rather than for physical characteristics. The birds on the facing page are "cover girls" from a popular British budgerigar book. They are very different from Miss Miller's "types." Miss Miller breeds budgies for pets, not for show. Photo by Dr. Herbert R. Axelrod.

foods is basically an egg mixture; take four pieces of ground Zwieback toast and thoroughly mix with an equally finely ground-up hard-boiled egg. This is then moistened by the addition of one finely ground carrot. Then the mixture is ready to be fed. To improve on this food one could also add some glucose powder, bread yeast and algal flour. There is little that can go wrong with it. However, one should never add more than a pinch (tip of knife) of bread yeast and algal flour, and glucose, at the most a teaspoonful. Once this nutritionally excellent food is being taken by the birds, the battle is virtually over.

Instead of Zwieback toast, many breeders use old (hard) ground-up bread rolls, sliced wheat bread or pieces of waffle. The hard-boiled eggs are often replaced with dehydrated egg powder or milk powder, and sometimes such substances as meat, fish or bone meal, finely ground-up insects or shrimp meal are also added to soft food mixtures. Using this, one assumes that budgerigars in the wild feed to some degree on insects. However, anything with a strong odor (like meat and/or fish meal) should be added in moderation only. Although there is a strong difference of opinion among academics as to whether birds can or cannot smell, the experienced budgerigar breeder knows that his birds will only feed very reluctantly or not at all on foul-smelling food.

There are also obvious visual preferences; invariably budgies accept more readily light-colored foods than darker colored ones. More recently baby foods and similar substances have been used very successfully in raising parakeets. After all, what is good for babies cannot possibly do any harm to birds either. Baby food, however, can be costly.

Many budgerigar breeders include a significant portion of oatmeal in their soft food mixtures. Cage bird fanciers and those who have only a small group of birds will probably prefer to use the relatively expensive brands designed for human consumption; however, animal feed oatmeal, available from wholesalers, sells for about 2/3 less and is equally nutritious. Breeders of the British show race of budgerigars should spare no expense to look after their birds. This highly specialized breed responds quickly and rather negatively to inadequate care and low quality food. Since one cannot really compare the quality-oriented breeding objectives for these highly priced birds with the mass breeding of common budgerigars, it is understandable that the specialized breeders invest more in time, money and effort in these expensive birds. On the other hand, some breeders obtain excellent breeding results by using commercially available dog meals for their birds.

Therefore, for reasons of quality, British breeders use milk instead of water, and milk is also used as the moistening agent in soft foods. Some German breeders have successfully copied this practice. However, this requires considerably more effort, particularly during the warm summer months or in the case of birds kept in warm rooms; under these circumstances milk turns sour very quickly, especially when used in soft foods. This can lead to serious gastro-intestinal problems for the birds.

When milk is being used it should be skimmed milk. Its protein content is as high as regular milk. Milk fat is neither required nor nutritionally beneficial for budgerigars. Regular milk can, of course, also be used, provided it is properly diluted. Under no circumstances should condensed milk be used, since its fat content equals that of heavy cream. Diluting this to an acceptable concentration is difficult and time-consuming. All containers used for milk and/or milk-enriched foods have to be washed daily in hot water. On very humid days, milk should only be offered during the early morning hours; it should be replaced with water at about noon.

Some breeders in England and on the continent are using—with surprisingly much success—bread rolls soaked in milk as rearing food, pressing out the excess milk just prior feeding. If only dry seeds are fed, and in the absence of any

The companionship of a budgerigar is, ounce for ounce, great! Budgies are clean, amusing, entertaining, easy to care for, inexpensive to buy and maintain and make the best gifts. Is it any wonder that almost 3,000,000 budgerigars were sold as pets worldwide in 1980?

green food or germinated seeds, budgerigars will also take bread rolls soaked in water to rear their young. Initially, this was the accepted method to mass-produce low-quality parakeets. This method has little, if anything, to do with being an animal lover, although parakeets appear to thrive even under these conditions. Yet, it is misleading, since birds raised this way appear bloated, have little energy and will succumb under the slightest physiological stress.

Germinated seeds are a conditioning and rearing food, which can be used throughout the year if need be, provided the birds are not too fat and as long as this food is not permitted to freeze. However, soft food is purely a rearing food, which is only given while young are being raised. Besides, most budgerigars will take this kind of food only during the breeding season.

Every breeder will have observed that the amount of soft food taken varies within each strain and between individual breeding pairs. If all essential foods are being made available, there is ultimately little difference between those young which have been reared with soft foods and those which have been given other foods.

Also quite useful as food supplements are tree bark, branches, twigs and buds. If a breeder has access to fruit trees he can give his birds a "treat" by giving them fresh branches, which usually carry buds from late winter on. Similarly useful are willow tree branches.

Small branches, secured in the upper third of the cage, will be totally chewed to pieces, and the buds, most of the bark and the soft wood marrow will be eagerly eaten. Large branches are usually completely de-barked by budgies. This sort of activity is most beneficial for the birds, because tree juices, as well as the tender buds, contain during the spring months nutritional substances which are essential. Moreover, seeing these colorful birds climb among the branches is indeed a delightful sight, and it is, of course, good exercise for the birds. Frequently replaced branches and twigs also keep the budgerigars off any wooden materials used to build the aviary. In spring, the budgie likes beech tree and birch tree branches, which at that time just begin to form buds. In addition, all other non-poisonous leafy branches can be used.

One of the best food supplements for budgies is a tree which has been freshly chopped down and has bark, insects and wood available for the budgie flock to eat. This tree has really been worked over!

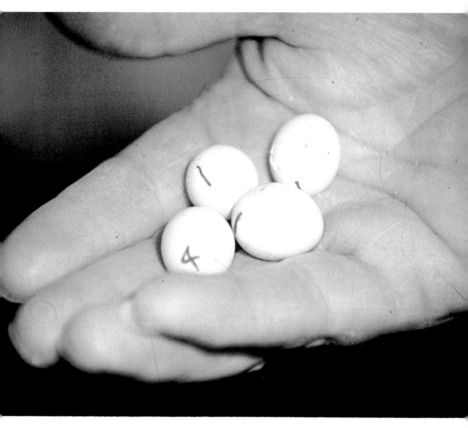

In the wilds of Australia small parrots such as the red-rumped parrot hen shown on the facing page nest in the hollows of trees—as does our popular budgerigar, which lays the small eggs shown above. The eggs were numbered by the breeder as they were laid, to indicate the order in which they should hatch. Photo of the eggs by Ray Hanson; Ken Stepnell photographed the parrot in Australia.

If you removed the top of a nest box, as did Dr. Axelrod to photograph a mother with her four chicks and four unhatched eggs, this is what you'd see.

Breeding

Most reference books will categorically state that nothing is easier than breeding budgerigars. This may be superficially true, because how else could this little Australian bird have become so inexpensive and so popular within 130 years? (It has been alleged that some people go to pet shops and ask for a parakeet to match their wall paper.) It happens over and over again that a single pair kept in a cage starts to breed without any special provisions being made for the birds. Invariably, such an event causes considerable headaches for the unsuspecting pet owner. Although common budgerigar "pets" do not have highly specific breeding requirements, the serious minded breeder, who places considerable importance on the well-being of his birds as well as running an economic breeding operation, must be familiar with certain basic fundamentals of budgerigar breeding.

It must also be said that, frequently, a cage bird fancier, who started out with a single pair which bred unexpectedly, eventually became a dedicated breeder. Quite often one sees aviaries, which obviously began as small structures, become larger and larger through repeated additions, eventually occupying almost the entire yard or garden. If there is also a well-cultivated patch of chickweed, then it is obvious that here lives a serious bird fancier.

Before embarking on breeding budgerigars, the breeder must give some thought to the eventual disposal of newly raised birds. Supply and demand very much determine the price to be obtained, and thus price fluctuations are to be expected. Therefore, it is, at best, risky to attempt to breed

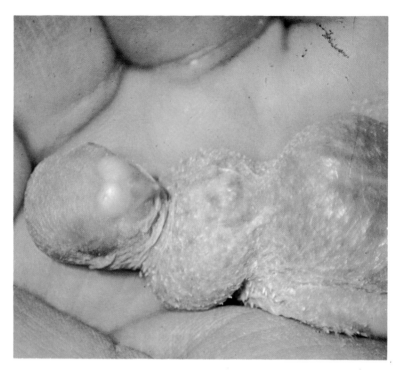

A new born chick, above, is just a bit too small to be banded. But the same chick three days later is the right size for the banding. Photos by Ray Hanson.

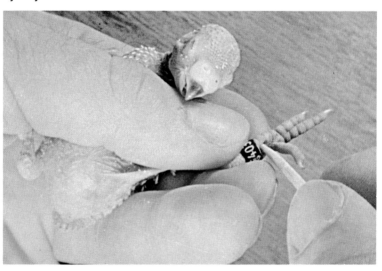

A few weeks later the chicks are covered with feathers, though they still must be fed by their parents. The photo below shows the birds just about ready to leave the nest.

budgerigars on a commercial basis. Breeding these birds as a hobby is far more fun. Anyone wanting to breed budgerigars for profit must keep at least 300 pairs in a continuous breeding cycle. He must also have a reliable dealer who buys the young birds, if he is to make any kind of satisfactory living from such a venture.

Anyone who has bred common parakeets for fun, and who wishes to get more deeply involved, should consider exhibiting show budgerigars. This then becomes, of course, an entirely different proposition. The initial investment is rather high, since the (now) serious breeder has to get into this field in a big way, or at least he has to start out with a few high quality pairs. Nowadays one pays a hefty price for one of the better birds, and prices for really fine specimens can be astronomical. The price of a common budgerigar of compatible colors, though, will be much less. Both types of bird require about the same amount of care and cost the same to feed.

Competition in the field of show and exhibition budgerigars has become increasingly intense in recent years. An added, complicating factor is that the strain of show budgerigars is, genetically, relatively young yet and, therefore, the birds do not always breed true. In other words, it is not enough to purchase two "top prize winners" in order to make a high quality breeding pair and expect to obtain offspring which are 100% show champion material again. I strongly urge any budding breeder to start small and purchase a few good birds instead of many of low quality.

BREEDING IN AVIARIES

Breeding in aviaries comes closest to the natural requirements of budgerigars as colony-breeding birds.

The number of birds per aviary (including an adjacent enclosed room or shelter area) is determined on the basis of 1 cubic meter per pair. Additional, unmated birds are little more than "trouble makers", particularly for breeding fe-

96

males. It is imperative that the entire colony be introduced into the aviary at the same time. Adding pairs at a later stage is often problematic, since they will be considered as "newcomers" by the well-established birds and fighting will often ensue. Moreover, it is important to provide more nest boxes than there are breeding pairs (ideally, at a ratio of 1:2).

The boxes should be attached at eye level in the sheltered area of the aviary, so that they can be easily inspected. It is not important that all the nest boxes be of the same shape or size and be at the same height. Parakeets often have individual preferences for particular nest boxes. Initially, there may be a fair amount of "arguing", particularly if two females are determined to occupy the same box, even though there may be another similarly suitable one close by. Fortunately, though, serious fighting is the exception rather than the rule. However, should this happen, the final outcome is often uncertain at the beginning. It can lead to the death of the "losing" female unless one or the other bird is quickly removed. Yet, a "compromise" is also possible. It has been reported that two females have nested in the same box, sharing both the male and the chicks. In such a case, the male will later on feed the nestlings from both females. However, under these circumstances, there are not usually many young. The lack of air circulation will cause some of the embryos to die. Therefore, if such an unusual "arrangement" is being observed, it is advisable to remove one female and the male, since the latter could turn into a "trouble maker" within the colony. Rivalry fights among males are uncommon; however, if they do happen blood is rarely spilled.

If all goes well the birds will pair off quickly; unfortunately, though, this does not always happen as the breeder has planned it from a genetic point of view. Undesirable pairing-off can be avoided when all respective partners are kept separated for two weeks prior to mating. Such isolation cages can be of a temporary nature, since the birds will soon be released into a larger flight area (aviary). Mating according to the plans and wishes of the breeder can be effected quicker when males and females have been kept separated for several weeks. This procedure tends to terminate early pair bonds and increases the readiness in both sexes to take on a new partner.

The first courtship approaches are made by the male. Making gurgling sounds, he beats against perches and the cage/aviary walls with his beak, turns nodding towards the female, and jumps up and down on the perch next to the female. With increasing excitement the male's pupils become contracted. If the female finds the courting male to be suitable, she too becomes excited and begins a similar dance. Her pupils too become contracted. In between, she begs for food—just like a chick—and the male will feed her by regurgitating food from his crop. Finally, the female squats down for copulation, which is intense and prolonged. Only during periods of sudden excitement early on in a courtship, *i.e.,* "love at first sight" syndrome, is the copulation quick and yet successful. The female drops its wings and raises its tail. It is then mounted by the male, which hangs onto the female's back and neck feathers with its claws and beak. Moving one wing around the female, the male slides down, towards the area of the cloaca, where, after prolonged thrusting, the sperm is transferred. A sure sign of a successful and completed copulation is when, afterwards, the female is fed by the male.

For increasingly prolonged periods the female will now go to its nest box. The formation of eggs is indicated by an increasing abdominal size. Females with a swollen, partially naked cloacal region and which display continuous tail whipping are just about to lay eggs.

Normally, it takes about eight to fourteen days from copulation to when the first egg is laid. However, this may take up to three or four weeks in females which are breeding for the first time, especially when they are already older than a year. If no eggs have appeared within five to six weeks, al-

98

though the female spends several hours daily in the nest box and the male acts normally during courtship, then something is wrong. It could be possible that the female cannot lay any eggs, or that through a deformed oviduct eggs are passed into the abdominal cavity. Should the latter happen, the eggs either become absorbed or a septicemia develops, with death rapidly following. Since budgerigars have become highly domesticated animals, such abnormalities are on the increase, especially among females from the heavy British race. It is fundamentally wrong to leave an apparently healthy but unproductive female for months together with males, hoping that this bird will eventually lay eggs. This places an energy drain and stress upon both female and male, and it is thus an obviously pointless effort. Sometimes, after an extended rest period such females actually do produce eggs, which are often dropped in flights. Sometimes, after a change of environment or partner, normal breeding will take place. However, since these are exceptions, it is often better for all concerned not to breed such birds but to give them away as pets. Unfortunately, they will not become as tame as those birds which have been kept alone most of their lives.

Completely infertile males are relatively rare. The reasons for unfertilized eggs vary; possible reasons include antipathy towards the partner and physiological complications (especially among older, heavier birds). To ensure successful copulations the breeder should provide sufficiently thick but not too smooth, properly fastened perches or branches. It must be remembered that budgerigars will never copulate on the ground or in a nest box. In birds with particularly dense plumage, fertilization can sometimes be promoted by carefully clipping the feathers around the cloacal opening in both partners. However, unfertilized eggs can also be the result of some deficiency in the female, or the embryos may have died. Only after several females have mated with the same male and all of them have produced infertile eggs can one safely assume that the male is sterile.

The nest-box concave holds eggs and newly hatched chicks (above). Because budgies do very little nest building, the concave helps keep eggs (and chicks) together (facing page). Because of the chicks' nakedness, they need their mother to keep them warm (below).

The key to breeding success with budgerigars is the condition of the breeding pair. This can be determined by a visual inspection of the birds' general appearance and careful observation of their behavior. Males in breeding condition have a bright blue nasal skin fold (cere), shiny eyes and are constantly "threatening" each other. Females have a dark brown cere and they behave similarly as the males toward each other. They are more active than usual, flying about noisily and chewing on every conceivable object. Later on lesbian unions are formed complete with all the rituals, such as courtship, feeding and copulation. Under optimum conditions this behavior lasts only a few weeks and it is relatively independent of the seasons. However, the breeding condition can indeed by adjusted through an increase of germinated seeds and through an increase in illumination time during the winter months. It requires a bit of experience to judge the right moment when both partners are in prime condition, be it in the winter or when breeding budgerigars throughout the whole year. However, when the sexes have been kept separated in an unheated room without additional illumination, there are no problems at all. Then within the seasonal cycle of European latitudes, budgerigars will without fail be ready to breed at the onset of spring. They will produce two to three clutches (more should not be permitted) in rapid succession and then go into their seasonal molt. In artificially-induced breeding, a reduced molt and a periodic partial loss of plumage are not necessarily a deterrent for successful breeding, as long as the birds are indeed in breeding condition.

A handful of fine wood sawdust, free of paint and other chemical additives, serves as a base for the nest. This gives some protection to the eggs by preventing them from rolling out of the nest. (They will not be incubated once they are outside the nest.) Some females remove some or all of the sawdust, preferring to lay their eggs on the bare wooden floor of the nesting box. Sawdust is essentially a substitute for the fine wood chips produced by the female when she carves out the nesting site inside a hollow tree. Apparently some females are more thorough than others when preparing the nest site. Most of the more attentive females pluck out some of their feathers and pad the nest with them just before the eggs are laid.

Generally speaking, eggs are laid every two days, some time between 3:00 p.m. and 4:00 p.m. It is important to remember this timing, because some birds, particularly females, tend to eat their eggs. Such a problem can be solved by quickly removing freshly laid eggs and replacing them with porcelain "dummy" eggs which are commercially available for canary breeders. Once habitual egg-eaters have hurt their beaks repeatedly on the hard, false eggs, they are usually broken of this habit. After that, such a bird can usually be trusted again with its own eggs to continue breeding. Incidentally, the periodic removal of eggs facilitates equal hatching of all eggs in a clutch. Therefore, some breeders routinely remove the first four or five eggs, which are then placed in clearly marked boxes and stored in a cool, well-ventilated place. It is important to remember to turn each egg daily, *i.e.*, to move it around its own axis so that the umbilical cord attached to the free-floating egg yolk is not torn. Eggs left in the nest are instinctively turned by the attending female. The method of routinely removing eggs, so that the entire clutch hatches at the same time, is not exactly as intended by nature, and it rarely pays to interfere with a natural breeding sequence. Newly hatched nestlings are fed, during the first few days of their lives, exclusively with a stomach secretion produced by the female, which includes predigested food substances. When feeding her young, the female is able to differentiate between the youngest nestlings, which receive only fore-stomach milk, and the oldest nestling (several days apart from the youngest), which receives mucus-coated seeds from the crop of the female. It is amazing how the female is able to distinguish the individual

A closeup of the hen budgie with her brood. Below: Both parents are required to feed the brood.

Because of their nakedness, the baby chicks need their mother to keep them warm. If neither their mother nor a foster mother is available, other arrangements must be made; if the chicks become severerely chilled they will die.

This nicely feathered pied chick is ready to be handled (see lower photo). The sooner it is handled, the easier it will be to train. If the chick learns to associate gentle handling and pleasant experiences (perhaps in the form of food rewards) with human company it will become much more amenable to training of all kinds.

nestlings in the darkness of the nest box. Here we have to remember that with four hatchlings the oldest is seven days older than the most recently hatched bird. With such age difference, the foot of the oldest nestling is as big as the entire newly hatched nestling. In clutches of six to eight eggs, which are quite common, the size disparities become even more grotesque. All nestlings are lying side-by-side and on top of each other inside the nest depression, with their heads pointing towards the middle of the nest. The female sits with her wings spread on top of the nestlings. In large broods of eight or more nestlings the smallest (youngest) bird occasionally gets squashed to death; however, this is relatively uncommon. When feeding her young, the female attends to each nestling individually, turning it on its back, grabbing its beak and administering exactly the right amount of food it needs according to its age.

At first the crop of the female is filled by the attending male. The oldest nestlings are fed first, the youngest last, when the crop is already empty. Then, through repeated retching efforts the fore-stomach milk is regurgitated. This is tremendous effort for such a small bird.

Now, through interference by the breeder, all nestlings are of about the same age and the female has to feed them initially with fore-stomach milk only, which is often insufficient in quanitity and of inferior quality. Similarly, older nestlings require the voluminous food, so that the crop filling may not be enough for one feeding. This then places additional stress on both adult birds. Although eager males will often participate in the feeding of their young from early age by slipping into the nest box, initially many females reject the entering males. Instead they insist that all food for the young passes through two crops, so they wait to be fed at the entrance to the nest box. If this is not fast enough they may even come outside and attack the male. If he still does not provide food as rapidly as the female needs it, she may even gather up the food herself, which of course requires more time, because the food has to be pre-digested first.

Therefore, if the eggs are not being eaten and if a clutch is not too large, one should really not interfere with the normal breeding sequence. Later on, the breeder can thin out some of the nests that have too many nestlings and add some to those with only a few. As long as the age difference is not too large, budgerigars will easily tolerate such manipulations. The general accounting, as far as the parentage is concerned, is easy as long as those young which are moved already carry a leg band.

Unfortunately, it is not too uncommon to find entire clutches which are infertile. In such a case one should not immediately remove the eggs so that the birds can start another clutch. Instead, they should be permitted to continue to incubate and at some later stage they should be given some nestlings from another pair. This method maintains the natural breeding rhythm.

One to two days before the first egg is laid, the female produces large amounts of feces, which is a sure sign of imminent egg laying. This phenomenon remains throughout the entire breeding cycle, a mechanism that enables the female to remain longer in the nest. Since these large droppings are always deposited at the same spot, they are easily removed.

Newly laid budgerigar eggs are chalk-white, with a faint pink transparency when held against light. After eight days of incubation fertile eggs take on a faint bluish sheen and become slightly darker. A trained eye (an experienced breeder) can spot this immediately. For those less experienced a gas stove lighter can become a handy tool to determine egg fertility. A flashlight bulb is installed at the upper end of the lighter (where the glowing wire is). Such a flexible light source can then be held among the eggs in a clutch; the darker, fertile eggs can easily be distinguished from the lighter, unfertile eggs. A fertile egg will appear reddish against the light (because of the blood vessels); then because of the growing embryo, it will turn darker, except the area where there is a small air bubble at the blunt end of the egg. Should the embryo die, the outer egg shell will become markedly dark or take on a spotty appearance. It may even become half dark and half light, because the dead embryo has collapsed inside. Such eggs will readily "standup" when they are rolled about. They must be removed immediately because there is an imminent danger that they may burst (because of gas formation) whereby decay bacteria are released, which can endanger the remainder of the brood.

Eggs which are not fertilized remain clear ("clear eggs"). There is little danger that they may burst; most likely they dry out. Such eggs should not be removed immediately, especially when one expects only a few hatchlings. The eggs tend to support the initially very tiny, totally helpless hatchlings, and they may well stop the female from squashing some of her nestlings. This danger is quite real in broods consisting of only one or two nestlings, particularly so with heavy females of the British race. When there is no damage to any internal organs the youngsters stay alive and appear to develop normally. However, at the latest after fourteen days the breeder will notice these (previously squashed youngsters) to be peculiarly flat with the legs spread in opposite directions. Upon close examination one can invariably determine a bent backbone. In the event that this has happened these birds should immediately and painlessly be destroyed, since they would develop into virtual cripples. The breeder slogan refers to such unfortunate birds as "frogs". It has so far not been determined whether this condition is caused by pressure onto a still soft skeletal structure, because "frogs" have also been noticed among normal, large broods. This then seems to suggest the possibility of a degeneration, for instance through attempts (by British breeders) to breed "oversize", which cannot keep pace with normal skeletal development.

Sometimes eggs are also damaged unintentionally by the adult birds. Small dents or cracks can easily be repaired with a piece of plastic tape, as long as the internal egg skin has not been damaged. The young of such repaired eggs will invariably hatch quite normally. However, once liquid has come out of an egg, or the air bubble inside becomes abnormally large, the egg is usually lost and tends to dry out.

Eyelid damage and beak deformities can also be sustained at the nestling stage, through action by adult birds. Their claws can inflict damage to eyes, and beak deformities can occur during feeding. There is little one can do to prevent eye damage; fortunately it happens very rarely. Deformities of the beak can indeed by avoided through regular visual inspections. Germinated seeds and soft food should be cleaned off before they can become caked-on and encrusted, which inhibits normal growth of the beak. This is especially true of wheat germ, which encrusts very quickly. A normal budgerigar beak has an upper beak growing over a lower beak; a deformed beak has the upper beak placed inside the projecting lower beak. Such deformed birds are later unable to feed their own young; at exhibitions they are automatically disqualified. So far, it has not been proved that such deformities are of genetic origin. If such a bird appears in a colony, it should definitely not be used for breeding. Instead, it would probably make a present as a pet to someone and thus lead a completely normal life.

There can be many reasons for embryos dying. The humidity in a breeding facility is, of course, of paramount importance. It must never be below 60% saturation, and a hygrometer is a worthwhile, not very expensive but essential investment. If the air is too dry it can lead to a contraction of the internal egg's skin, thus tightly enclosing the embryo so that it simply cannot hatch out. A young bird inside an egg has to make his first decisive effort when hatching. It must make revolving movements inside the egg and thus "saw" through the shell along the entire upper third of the egg with an "egg tooth" attached to its beak (the egg tooth is lost shortly after hatching). This is followed by strong shoulder movements which lift the sawed-through section of the shell. After that the young nestling takes its first few breaths of air and then rests after this enormous physical effort. During that time the lower portion of the new chick, still inside the egg's shell, dries out and the remainder of the shell detaches itself automatically. Only then will the female help by removing the empty shells from the nest and out of the nest box proper.

Some embryos are simply too weak to struggle out of their shells, or they may even die before they get to that stage. It has been shown that breeding birds, which were either too young, too old, not healthy or which had been bred too often (at the most one should attempt three broods per year) have a poor fertility or hatching record. Ultimately, it has to be remembered that the egg-producing female can only put into her eggs what she has available in terms of energy reserves.

The modern strains of the British budgerigar race can become endangered during the hatching phase because of constant attempts to breed birds with larger heads. As it is, the head is already the largest part of an embryo. An excessively large head could prevent the parakeet embryo from making the necessary movements inside the egg and thus contribute to its premature death. Increasing embryo mortality is a proven fact among the highly bred British race.

If the budgerigar baby is alive and well, one can hear its voice from the seventeenth incubation day on inside the egg. It is a continuous, drawn-out chirping sound, which—after hatching—even penetrates through the walls of the nest box to the outside. This sound is the signal for the female to feed this youngster for the first time. The breeder can recognize this externally by the slight yellowish enlargement of the neck. He can then expect a normal development of the brood. Some females have, at first, no fore-stomach milk or simply do not feed their first-born. Such unfortunate

110

young birds will continue to chirp for hours; yet their crops remain empty. If they cannot be transferred to the nest of another breeding female within twelve hours, they will die.

The remainder of the yolk sac will be drawn into the embryo's body during the last few hours prior to hatching, so that any newly hatched bird can draw on this energy reserve before it is fed by the female. Young canaries can live up to three days off their yolk sac; however, budgerigars with their high metabolic rate have a shorter energy supply.

Most young, inexperienced females which have not fed their young immediately will feed without fail once they have been given one or two older (four to six days old) nestlings. These youngsters are more persistent with their calls, which act as a stronger stimulus to induce proper maternal behavior. Besides, such advanced nestlings can already take some pre-digested food in addition to fore-stomach milk. These females invariably begin to feed normally with their next brood.

The majority of budgerigars including the highly bred "pedigree" strains are very good parents. Most males will attempt to help feed their young right from the start. In fact, many will even attempt to help with the incubating, as long as the female permits it. Not every female will permit the male to enter the nest box; on the other hand, some may even enjoy it and will move over to give the male some room. Both extremes have advantages and disadvantages. The eggs and small nestlings may be damaged and injured when both parent birds are continuously inside the nest box; however, the young are invariably fed better and more promptly.

A newly hatched budgerigar is at first nearly naked and blind. Its eyes are only recognizable as two dark patches on both sides of the head. Red-eyed and cinnamon-colored budgerigars have eye patches which are lighter or of a reddish coloration, a characteristic which distinguishes these strains right from the moment of hatching. The body of a baby budgie has only tiny erect down feathers, which

The young budgies shown above are the product of an Australian pied hen and a normal olive green cock. The photo on the facing page shows the same birds before their feathers were fully grown: short flights and feather sheaths are still visible. Photos by Harry V. Lacey.

grow rapidly. After about eight days most of the body is covered with a fluffy down cover. Normal-colored budgerigars have mouse-gray down plumage; lighter-colored strains including the opaline budgerigars have a white down plumage. This enables the breeder of mixed color strains to make preliminary determinations from the color of the down plumage. At the same time the feather tracts appear, together with the stalks of mature wing feathers and tail feathers. These are, depending on the color of the strain, either dark, light or mixed. Young calicos, for instance, show very early which wing and tail feathers will remain dark and which will become light.

It takes two weeks until the regular color plumage appears from underneath the by now rather thick downy cover. Until that time, young budgerigars look more like young birds of prey than parrots.

At the age of three weeks the nestlings begin to look more like budgerigars. At that time the wing and tail feathers break out of their stalks, and the original, somewhat spiny appearance due to the feather stalks begins to be replaced with the shiny and smooth budgie plumage.

Some time between the fourth and fifth weeks, the day of the nestlings' departure from the nest comes. This imminent event can be recognized by a peculiar sound through the nest box walls, which resembles the humming of tiny airplane propellers . . . the young are exercising their wings, a practice referred to by breeders as "propellering". These exercises strengthen the wing muscles of the young birds; they are doing them instinctively in the darkness of the nest box, without the parents having to show them.

Strangely enough, by the thirtieth day any of the earlier on previously observed, age-dependent, size and growth disparities of the first three of four nestlings have disappeared. However, among large broods the youngest birds are usually not quite ready yet, when the oldest ones have already begun leaving the nest box. Moreover, it is usually the oldest nestling which makes the first flight attempts. This youngster sits then usually for some time on the interior nest box perch, inside the entrance hole, looking out. After several attempts it eventually flies off. The next youngsters take off more quickly. Once they are in the aviary they rarely ever return to their nest.

At first, the young birds land on the ground. Although they can fly, it is the landing which still requires practice. However, within a few days they fly about in the aviary just as swiftly as their parents. Once in the aviary, they will also start immediately to pick up seeds, yet the male will continue to feed them for another eight to fourteen days, at first still regularly and later on at a steadily declining rate. It is also the adult male which tends to coax the youngsters to the feed container or seed dispenser.

The adult female pays no attention once her brood has left. In fact, freshly laid eggs appear in the nest again even before the last nestling has gone. This can cause some problems, although there is very little one can do about it. Sometimes, females simply throw the remaining nestlings out of the nest, which can cause some injuries, particularly if the youngsters resist such forceful removal. The more tolerant female will put up with stragglers which, during their wing exercises, can possibly damage some of the new eggs of the next clutch. This is one of the disadvantages of aviary breeding, and there is very little a breeder can do about it. With an increased overall productivity in aviary breeding such minor disadvantages are always overcome.

Only a few budgerigars ever remove the feces of the young from the nest box. This presents no problem, because in healthy broods the droppings will harden quickly to form dry, odorless balls. These allegedly contain certain antibiotics and thus they should not be removed. Yet, there are also those adult birds which feed a lot of wet food, so that their young excrete a sort of mush feces without ever causing any disease problems. The nest of such birds should be cleaned regularly by the breeder, and frequently fresh sawdust should be added; at the same time the beaks and feet of the nestlings should be cleaned. With such birds it is pointless to withhold green food and soft foods; "wet feeders" will simply take in more water in order to keep the food for their youngsters more fluid. However, these birds should not be given milk. This if taken in excess by both nestlings and adults can cause diarrhea; instead water should be carefully rationed.

Freshly laid eggs which have become soiled by the feces of the previous brood, in particular the last few eggs of a very large clutch, should be carefully washed—holding the eggs between fingertips—in lukewarm water. Sometimes this procedure has to be repeated several times if the young are expected to hatch.

By the way, it is advantageous to float budgerigar eggs one to two days prior to hatching in lukewarm water for a little while. The moisture entering the eggs via shell pores softens the dried out internal egg skin, which facilitates easier hatching. There is no danger that the embryos drown; eggs in an advanced developmental stage will float at the surface and thus remain partially exposed to air. It is, however, of paramount importance that the water be neither too cold nor too warm, and the entire procedure should not take more than one to two minutes.

To produce one brood takes a total of about two months. In an aviary situation the youngsters from one brood can remain in the same enclosure until those from the next brood leave their nest. This aviary must, of course, be sufficiently large and not be too crowded. Birds destined for sale can be removed at an age of about six weeks. When they are removed from the aviary with skill and experience there should be no difficulty. The young birds, which are not yet experienced flyers, can easily be caught with a suitable bird net. This net should consist of a cloth-wrapped wire frame, which is covered with a shallow sack of sturdy netting material. It is important that any bird caught in the net be spotted immediately (the netting material must be quite transparent) and be removed from the net without delay. Attempts to catch more than one bird at a time might have serious consequences for the bird already in the net. The net handle must be flexible and not too long. Commercially available nets have a handle which is usually too short for use in larger aviaries. Incidentally, it is less dangerous to let a bird fly into the net, rather than to lash out after a bird clinging against the wire. Such a bird, trying to avoid the approaching net, sometimes gets partially caught and pressed against the wire, which can lead to serious injuries even if the net hoop is sufficiently padded.

If three successive broods are being raised, those from the first one should be removed and transferred to separate cages without nest boxes by the time the third one starts up. The reason for this is that under optimum conditions during the summer even these youngsters become sexually active. Particularly among young females there is a danger that they might invade nest boxes already occupied. However, the adult females in these boxes usually take a rather dim view of this, attacking the younger bird by aiming at the head of the invader. Quite often this happens with such violence that the skull of the invading bird is cracked. The young bird invariably lacks the experience to take advantage of the fact that it is coming from above. Even sub-adult males which are strongly "displaying" tend to disturb breeding adult pairs. However, among males—young and old—there rarely is ever any serious injury.

An extraordinary phenomenon are females which virtually "run amok". Although these are real rarities, they nevertheless can virtually wipe out all breeding activities in a particular aviary. Such females, which have invariably been a failure with their own broods, will without the slightest provocation go from one nest box to the next and attack the incubating females, destroy the eggs or massacre the nestlings.

Sometimes they destroy much promising brood material before they are stopped. After such a destructive excursion the attacking female usually returns to her own nest box, so that it is sometimes difficult to find out which one the offender really is. The damage can be even worse if the breeder is absent for some time. Of course, such females must be removed without delay and should not be used for breeding purposes again. Unfortunately, males are of little help, since they do not defend a territory or their own family.

Once the third brood has left the nest, the time has come to terminate the breeding activities for the year. Breeding pairs will have been breeding continuously for nearly six months. This is easier said than done, since not all pairs started their breeding cycle at the same time, and within six months the individual breeding sequences have further extended the overall breeding season. For instance, some pairs will have completed their third brood already, while some of the "straggling pairs" are just beginning to lay eggs for the third time. This situation can only be remedied through a systematic and rigorous intervention on the part of the breeder. Healthy budgerigars simply do not stop breeding. The limiting biological factor—lack of food in the Australian bush—is, of course, absent in captivity. Therefore, the only sure way to terminate the breeding cycle after the third brood is by removing individual pairs as soon as the third brood has left the nest, even if a fourth clutch of eggs is already present. These have to be either destroyed or—if they are from very valuable birds—can be added to other females still incubating.

Those pairs which have finished breeding should be transferred into separate aviaries for males and females. They can also be added to aviaries housing the young budgerigars, as long as breeding boxes are not being provided. Although some females will still drop one or two eggs, this does not have any significant effect on these birds. If there is a lack of suitable space, these pairs can be left together, as long as the nest boxes are removed and out of sight. Many breeders consider this method to be a more natural one and better for the birds. High-energy foods are eliminated, which invariably induces a complete molt. The ceres in both sexes become paler—a sure sign that the reproductive glands are regressing—and the birds begin to settle down. However, the breeder should maintain roughly an equal ratio of males and females in the aviary.

The breeding aviaries and all other equipment are now thoroughly cleaned, possibly disinfected and any parasites (mites) are destroyed with a suitable insecticide spray. Then, in the event of a year-round operation these aviaries can be occupied again. If the aviary has a natural top soil floor, this is dug up and turned over. One-half of the floor should be covered with fresh sand.

BREEDING IN CAGES

Although breeding budgerigars in individual cages requires more work and effort, it is still the preferred method in large commercial hatcheries. This method enables a more intensive production and affords better control. Cage dimensions and equipment have already been discussed in detail. It is imperative, however, that the breeding birds be kept separated into males and females for at least fourteen days in large, spacious aviaries before they are introduced into the breeding cages. This promotes an early onset of the breeding cycle. It is not uncommon to see budgerigars which are in prime breeding condition mate virtually immediately after they have been introduced into the breeding cage. These pairs will inevitably produce the first egg within eight days. Young females will require at least fourteen days, and after three weeks most of the pairs should have produced eggs. Should this require a longer period of time it is possible that there are some problems—either in antipathy between the partners, morphological or physiological difficulties, etc. It is important that the birds be closely monitored during this period. If certain pairs have not produced any eggs within six weeks, it is advisable to exchange partners. Alternately, these birds are returned to the aviary to obtain a better breeding condition. The periodic separation under the influence of sunshine and the open air sometimes produces miracles, although these cannot correct any organic damage which might exist. The normal breeding sequence in single cages corresponds to colony breeding in aviaries. It is advisable to have pairs accommodated in adjacent cages to permit visual contact. Besides, most pairs in a breeding facility maintain vocal contact with each other.

Budgerigar vocalization is indeed very loud. In contrast to colony breeding, mutual disturbances are eliminated by the use of individual breeding cages. All feedings can be individually adjusted, and it is immaterial for the overall operation when the individual pairs begin to breed. This method guarantees maintenance of the genetic basis, since there is close control over which birds are being mates, something which is impossible to maintain in an aviary. In a colony breeding situation some males will mate with more than one female. Unfortunately, budgerigars seem to have different selective criteria as far as their partner is concerned than the breeder. Even in individual breeding cages it has been observed that two adjacent pairs were determined to cross-breed. Those individual birds, which are trying to get to each other, tend to hang on the separating wire and maintain beak contact as well as feeding each other through the wires. However, the intended partner is invariably being attacked. Such a problem can only be alleviated through separation (to move out of sight) and exchange with a properly mated pair. Such an example of close pair bond acts as a stimulus, so that an initial antipathy turns to a mutual sympathy. It is also a good method to stimulate mated pairs which have not started to breed. There are, however, instances where intended partners have such a strong and deep-seated antipathy for each other that they will simply not breed, or the female will lay eggs and incubate them but will treat the male as an intruder who is to be attacked or even killed. This may also happen with females who have approached males without being accepted.

The advantages and disadvantages of nest boxes placed either inside the cage or attached from the outside have, however, already been discussed. It is easier to monitor nest boxes attached on the outside of the cage, and birds usually do not exhibit any preference. It is also easier to attach record cards on the outside of breeding boxes, which contain details about egg laying, onset of incubation, dates of hatching, leg band numbers of breeding pair and those leg band numbers intended for the nestlings. If larger record cards are used, one could include data about the genetic heritage of the breeding pair, its characteristics, coloration, and appearance of nestlings. These cards can be filed later on and thus additional bookkeeping work is avoided. Nest boxes attached to the inside of the cage simply do not lend themselves to an attachment of record cards, which would then be damaged by chewing and become soiled.

Very serious-minded breeders mark the eggs as they are being laid, giving them sequential numbers. A soft felt-tip pen is very useful for that purpose. This method enables an exact control of how many eggs are fertilized and infertilized. Moreover, it is then also possible to determine exactly the hatching date of each egg. Some breeders even mark the back of the naked nestlings, using, very cautiously, a felt pen. Using this method one can transfer nestlings, which have not yet been banded, without jeopardizing the genetic sequence.

Generally speaking, nestlings from cage broods leave the nest box somewhat earlier than those born in aviaries. This is of little consequence because there is less danger in a small cage for them to sustain any damage. Sometimes they will then remain, for the first few days, in one corner of the cage and sleep there in close body contact, as they did inside the nest box. During this time they look as if they are dead, lying on their sides. As one would expect, this is a bit of a terrifying sight for the beginning breeder. Most young budgerigars sleep relatively much during the day up to their eighth week. When they are sleeping on a perch they usually rest on both legs, which an old budgie will only do when it is not feeling very well. The early weaning of the young is the advantage with the breeding box, since it is available for the next brood that much sooner. The only drawback is that some youngsters—particularly females—have a tendency, after some days, to return to the adult female in the nest when they become tired. Some adult females will tolerate this; others, however, may attack the young to the point where they may be hurt. Generally speaking, the young from cage broods should not remain for more than two weeks with their parents, particularly so when another brood is expected. The youngsters will disturb the pair during its courtship and during copulation and thus fertilization of the eggs could conceivably be prevented. Besides, at this stage the young birds may at times be seriously attacked by both adult birds, so that they have to be removed quickly. Some adult females may even pursue the youngsters after they have flown away, hitting them dangerously on the head with their beaks. The young will have to be immediately removed, even if they are not weaned completely yet. This is a distinct disadvantage of cage breeding. Young budgerigars will begin feeding by themselves far quicker than any other young birds, even if they are still strongly begging for food.

Newly weaned budgerigars raised in cages should not be immediately transferred to aviaries. They are still too clumsy and inexperienced. Ideally, they are first accommodated in transition cages which are maintained at eye level. For that purpose, one can use empty breeding cages or unused flight cages. It is important that the birds can find food and water, that they have sufficient perches and at least some flight space. Contact with the keeper must be maintained so that the birds remain tame and can be easily observed.

Important for those breeders who are primarily interested in the mass producing of birds is the disposal of newly weaned budgerigars for taming. Therefore, in such transition cages potential customers can take their time in selecting a bird. For the exhibition breeder this is the best time for preliminary training, since the young bird is at a very impressionable age. Therefore, training cages should be interconnected by a small gate with the already mentioned exhibition cages; the young bird is then occasionally coaxed with some spray millet into the exhibition cage for a short period of time.

It is advisable that the breeder spend a little bit of time each day with these young birds, by talking to them and by very gently coaxing them, with the aid of a little stick, to fly from one perch to the other without unduly scaring them. Most young birds at this age are still so naturally uninhibited that they would bite the stick rather than flee from it; this is something the bird will then later on never forget. Those who wish to acquire a tame "talker" are usually grateful for such a pre-tamed bird. Therefore, young budgerigars which have been raised in cages should be kept three to four weeks in such training cages. Those birds destined for sale should not be introduced into an aviary at all. If there are already a few slightly older birds in these training cages then it is usually very easy to add some which have been kicked out of the nest by their parents prematurely. The older birds will virtually "adopt" the younger ones and then feed them, when the young beg persistently enough (incidentally, old breeding males may also serve that purpose). If a breeder has the time, the pre-taming process can already begin when the young are still in the nest box. From the third week on they can be removed individually every day, placed in the palm of a hand and petted with the other hand. Most nestlings will sit very quietly with the eyes closed in obvious enjoyment, or alternately crawl into the sleeve, where they like to settle down. However, sometimes females, even at this early stage, can give painful bites. This is one thing one simply has to endure.

It is also important for cage breeding that the adult birds feel comfortable. This can be achieved easier in breeding boxes than in aviaries. Sometimes one encounters naturally shy birds or those which have been ruined as youngsters. Such birds, particularly females, tend to continuously screech as soon as somebody approaches the nest box. Later on the nestlings imitate this, even when they have been flying for several days. They will panic as soon as somebody approaches the cage. This problem can only be resolved with patience and tender loving care, and even then some birds will never become really tame. These individuals rarely can be effectively shown in exhibition cages.

Cleanliness has to be more thoroughly applied to cage breeding than to aviary breeding in order to prevent diseases and avoid parasites. After each brood, the nest boxes have to be cleaned, even when there are already eggs in the nest again (something which will nearly always be the case). After the eggs have been gently removed—they are kept in a safe, warm place—the entire box and the nest depression are thoroughly cleaned and a handful of fresh sawdust as well as a few feathers from the females are added. It is important for some of the more sensitive females that the feathers in the nest be their own; the breeder can easily pick these up off the cage bottom. Under these conditions, the female is rarely disturbed and will immediately resume incubation. However, some females may well react adversely and, for instance, may throw out all the new sawdust as well as their own newly laid eggs, which because of the change have become foreign debris.

Mites are not as dangerous to budgerigars as they are, for instance, to canaries, yet these parasites can cause significant problems. The red bird mite is a tiny, to the naked eye barely visible, insect. It produces prolifically during hot dry summer weather and it has easy access to all bird accommodations, without actually having to be transmitted by birds. It is, therefore, no disgrace to a breeder when mites are present; however, it is more reprehensible if nothing is done about it. During the day these parasites hide in cracks and other spaces, and during the night they attack the birds, sucking their blood. During periods of warm weather the mites reproduce rapidly, but they can also survive for weeks during periods of cold and lack of food. Mites which have taken on their fill of blood are clearly recognizable as red spots.

Mites do not represent a serious danger to adult birds; however, they can weaken them, and they are a strong irritant, particularly to incubating females. Newly hatched nestlings can be killed within one night by blood-sucking mites when these are permitted to increase rapidly. Therefore, the breeder has to be constantly alert to the presence of mites and institute prophylactic measures. These should include spraying of the nest boxes, cages and all equipment with an effective mite spray. It need not be stressed that if a mite spray is used it must not affect the birds. There are a number of substances commercially available which, according to the manufacturer, do not adversely affect birds. These substances can be applied through brushing in cracks and all other spaces where mites tend to hide during the day. Particular attention has to be paid that feed and water containers are kept away from these chemicals.

More recently, so-called pest strips have been used quite successfully. These are plastic-like strips which are suspended from ceilings in apartments to destroy flies and mosquitos. Allegedly they kill all mites within a few days if used in bird rooms, aviaries and cages. In fact, enclosures treated with pest strips will remain free of mites for months. There is little known about any detrimental effects to the birds. Of course, such strips must never be used in a room with meal-worm or other food insect cultures. The invisible vapors emitted by the strips kill all insects. They should also be placed sufficiently far away from nesting boxes. Budgerigars suffer little from other ectoparasites, since they can remove these cleverly with their own beaks.

Once a pair has produced two or three broods, the female and the nest box are removed immediately after the last nest-ling has flown out. Nonetheless, the male is kept together with the youngsters in the breeding cage until the brood becomes independent.

All females which have finished breeding are placed in a roomy flight cage or aviary. There, without the presence of males, they get along reasonably well with each other and will recover quickly. The males are similarly accommodated once the youngsters are on their own.

After the training period, those youngsters not to be sold are then transferred to the resting aviaries to join the males and females. Alternatively, they can also be placed in special aviaries for young birds only. This is merely a question of suitable space, based upon the measurements previously in-dicated for a breeding battery of cages and two aviaries. It is essentially a matter of opinion whether the resting birds and the young birds are kept—outside the breeding season—-segregated according to sexes. One school of thought teaches that the birds get better rest when separated by sex (even the young birds allegedly develop better under such conditions), while the other one considers it to be against the laws of nature and thus not desirable. It is argued that males and females do not get as fat when they are kept together. Moreover, it is not considered detrimental for the young birds to become sexually active very early on; in fact, such youngsters are expected to become better breeding birds later on. No doubt, both methods have their advantages and disadvantages. In any event, the sexes should be separated a few weeks prior to the onset of the breeding season, so that all pair-bonds established previously in the aviary are terminated and so that the formation of new bonds is not unnecessarily delayed.

It has happened repeatedly that budgerigars without a nest box have prepared nests in some corner of the aviary or even in burrows in the soil. This weakens the animals unnecessarily. The internal drive to chew on things among females ready to breed can lead to aviary damage, and birds can possibly escape. In my experience, keeping males and females together in large, roomy aviaries outside the breeding season maintains the birds in prime condition.

A beautiful, clean aviary in which quality budgerigars are raised.

Is a budgerigar really happy living in a cage? No one knows if they are but they seem to live much longer than those allowed to fly free subject to bad weather and enemies like hawks, cats and air rifles!

Free Living Budgerigars

As early as the last century people attempted to keep budgerigars free living in large private parks. Unfortunately, all of these experiments ended with the birds finally disappearing, although there were some initial preliminary successes.

The first one to succeed was the Duke of Bedford who managed to keep free living parakeets on his estate in the 1950's. Since then his method has been used on the estates of other British nobility as well as at the animal park at Whipsnade, near London. Apart from being suitably situated in a rural area, which must also be free of predators, one of the main prerequisites is a specially-constructed aviary. Essentially, such an aviary has to be positioned in a very protected area and yet afford adequate visual control. A most advantageous location is a large lawn area surrounded by trees, with one tree almost adjacent to the bird enclosure. This tree should be much taller than the aviary.

An aviary constructed and situated in this manner gives the birds proper orientation, because their homing instinct is limited, *i.e.,* it has to be re-established again after having been in captivity for so long. The aviary as such varies little from other facilities of this kind. The upper third of all sides of the outer flight cage should be protected with boards. This, too, affords better orientation from above and prevents the budgerigars from flying against the wire mesh. The wire ceiling of this aviary has to have a cut-out section about one meter square. The margins of this opening have to be structurally strengthened and support a hatch cover, which is controlled by an attached rope (similar to pigeon lofts). At the interior of the flight cage and attached to the opening is a funnel-shaped wire tunnel pointing downward. This wire tunnel is terminated a few centimeters above a large square food table, where there are always fresh seeds available. Whether the feed is in large containers placed on the table or simply scattered all over does not make any difference. Possibly such a table can have an elevated border frame around it.

When the hatch cover is open, the food is in plain sight and attracts the hungry homing parakeets. At first the approaching birds will land in the tree, go from there to the aviary roof and finally climb down the tunnel towards the food table. This returns them to the safe environment of the aviary, which is closed in the evening and on days with bad weather.

Early each spring ten robust young pairs, which have been kept in outside aviaries, are introduced into the free-flight cage. It does not need to be pointed out that one should use common parakeets instead of highly sensitive exhibition birds. The hatch cover remains closed until all females are breeding on well-established nests in nest boxes located in the protected area adjacent to the free-flight cage. It may even be better to keep the birds confined until the first nestlings have hatched. Then one morning the hatch is carefully opened. The narrow funnel entrance above the food table prevents a sudden mass escape if the birds become frightened (as is quite common among budgerigars). At first, some of the more daring males will cautiously move up through the narrow funnel opening and explore the immediate surroundings. During the first few days they rarely venture beyond the adjacent tree (besides, males, which have incubating females, will never go beyond the range of vocal contact). Once the birds become more accustomed to this new situation, the group of males will soon make further excursion flights. At first, the birds will fly in groups above the aviary and soon will settle down among the trees bordering the lawn area. From among the grass they will pick up various green foods and other tempting natural seeds, so that they will return, with their crops filled, to the incubating females. During this period one would rarely expect any losses to the colony (as long as there is not the occasional bird of prey; stray cats will have to be kept away from the aviary). Once the nestlings have flown out they are taken outside under the leadership of the males, which are now very familiar with the surroundings. Similarly the entire flock returns to the aviary as soon as they become hungry, although the excursion flights are now further away from the aviary to cultivated farmlands.

In our latitudes the budgerigars can only find food in an emergency for some weeks, and such an emergency does not really exist for these birds since they have been fed regularly right from the start. The breeding females rarely fly out of the aviary, and if they do, only for short flights. The contact to the nest box is stronger than their food drive. Losses among young birds are not greater than under normal conditions, and their development leaves nothing to be desired. Those breeders who do not wish to take any chances can keep the hatch cover closed at the end of the breeding season, until the next one. The raised young birds are disposed of as usual. Advertisements in British journals frequently offer "homing parakeets." Allegedly, such budgerigars come from free-flying colonies which easily adapt to the conditions at a new location. Some British free-flight cages are left open throughout the year. Under these conditions one can expect larger losses because of birds not returning for a variety of reasons. However, the owner of such a facility has, of course, the pleasure to observe these colorful parrots flying about freely throughout the year. These birds, with their incredibly swift and maneuverable flight, display some magnificent aerial acrobatics, while they spend their social hours huddled together in bushes and trees. Some flocks will land at a nearby stream to drink or to bathe while the individual birds of another one climb about tall grass reeds looking for seeds. It is not a rarity to find breeding birds in old hollow trees—the entire life of such free living budgerigars takes place in a totally natural environment, and they only return to the food table to feed on preferred millet seeds. This additional food supply should always be available to the birds. It facilitates a certain amount of control and, moreover, the aviary can temporarily be closed if the birds should decide to leave for good. The migration of budgerigars, as was noted above, is not restricted to a particular season. The symptoms are considerable nervousness among the birds, together with loud vocalizing. This happens only when there are no more eggs or young in the nest boxes. If the critical moment passes unnoticed the entire block may disappear without ever coming back. This migratory instinct among free living budgerigars which receive regularly additional food can lay dormant for a year or more only to return suddenly and unexpectedly. If the birds actually raised in such an aviary have been banded, there is hope at least some of them can be returned after they have become lost. However, prevention is still the best method.

Preferably, one should select dark colors, particularly green, for birds accommodated in such free-flight aviaries. Although light colored birds look very pretty, they invariably become easy prey for larger birds and other predators. They are very conspicuous and fall easy prey when pursued by a predator. On the other hand, green is a satisfactory protective coloration even in the European environment. Similarly dark blue birds are less endangered than white or yellow ones. Unfortunately, keeping free-flying parakeets can only be afforded by a few. Hobbyists should be cautioned against improvised attempts of this nature in densely settled urban areas; invariably they will end in disaster.

Diseases—Prevention and Treatments

There are few veterinarians who are specialized in the treatment of birds. Moreover, in something as small as budgerigars even the correct diagnosis is already a substantial problem. An immediate and proper treatment is imperative because a budgerigar which has not eaten for twenty-four hours will invariably die. Therefore, in order to prevent diseases it is important that the correct care, maintenance and food be provided.

Sick parakeets can be recognized by their lethargic behavior and dim eyes. When this happens even older birds sit on both of their legs. Their plumage, particularly the back feathers, is fluffed up and the neck is withdrawn into the shoulder. Diarrhea, recognizable by wet and dirty feathers around the anal opening, is a sure sign of a disease being present.

Many diseases are manifested by the regurgitation of seed grains accompanied by shaking head movements. Very sick birds are so weak that they spend most of the day sleeping with their head tucked under one wing. They either refuse food altogether or poke around in the food container listlessly. A bird showing these symptoms must be isolated and kept fairly warm immediately. Very suitable as an isolation cage is an old exhibition or training cage which has been equipped with an infra-red lamp or some other radiator. Cobs of spray millet should be attached to the wire. This is an easily digested food which is good for sick birds. Such a "treat" often persuades a very sick bird to resume feeding again. In less serious disease problems this procedure may be all that is required; however, if there is no improvement within the next few hours, a proper diagnosis is needed in order to determine a correct treatment.

A "cold" is caused predominantly by drafts or wetness, something which happens frequently during the wet-cold fall and winter months. Gastro-intestinal problems usually occur during the summer months after spoiled green food or too much fresh grass seeds have been fed. Young birds get sick easier than older ones; weakened older birds are more susceptible than those which have had an opportunity to rest. All birds are very susceptible to diseases during their main molt in the fall. The best prophylactic is a variable diet, sufficient calcium supplement and cleanliness.

Exhibitions also are a potential danger for infections and diseases through stress. Therefore, concerned exhibition committees usually add disinfectants to the drinking water, and provide draft-free well-ventilated transportation facilities and show accommodations which are neither too warm nor too cold. Yet, despite such care, problems do occur, and many hopeful exhibitors have returned with sick birds instead of first-prize ribbons.

Before budgerigars are taken on a trip they have to be fully fit. After they have been returned they should not immediately be placed into an aviary again. Instead they should be kept in cages indoors and with nourishing food for observation for a few days. Once it has been determined that there are no health problems, the birds are returned to their aviary. This same quarantine procedure should also be applied to newly purchased birds which arrive by rail transport.

PSITTACOSIS—THE NIGHTMARE
FOR BUDGERIGAR FANCIERS

Rarely has any other disease, which is transmittable from animals to humans, caused so much fear as the so-called parrot disease or psittacosis. In Germany, at the beginning of the 1930's, people who had been in contact with newly imported parrots came down with an initially mysterious disease. It resembled a serious pneumonia and ended—in many cases—in death. The pathogen was a virus, carried by parrots from tropical regions and transmitted to humans. In Germany this led to an enactment of laws in 1936 prohibiting all parrot imports and subjecting those birds already in the country to strict controls. All breeders and dealers had to keep detailed records about the origin of their birds, breeding results, disposal of captive bred birds, sale, deaths, etc., which were checked regularly by the Health Department. All parrots and budgerigars were required to have special leg bands with officially registered serial numbers, which had to be maintained in the respective records. Any source of subsequent outbreaks of psittacosis could thus be quickly established, and the offending birds could be destroyed.

Since budgerigars were the most commonly kept parrots and as pets have particularly close contact with humans, it was mostly this bird which caused human infections with psittacosis. Nowadays medical science has, fortunately, produced medications which have reduced the human fatalities enormously. Moreover, this disease is equally easily and effectively treated in birds without the entire stock having to be destroyed. In addition, research in the United States and Europe during the last few decades has shown that the psittacosis virus was in these regions anyway, and that it could be transmitted via other bird species to humans. This included feral house pigeons, turtle doves, sparrows and even domestic poultry. In the United States poultry workers have contracted the disease, and in Europe, people working in butcher shops carrying poultry, pigeon breeders, and inevitably pet shop staff have contracted psittacosis. However, this disease is rather rare among fanciers and other private establishments.

Since this disease is also transmitted by other birds, the name parrot disease has really become meaningless. Nowadays, one refers to it more generally as *ornithosis*. However, it has been observed that the virus transmitted by parrots is more virulent than that from other bird species.

In humans this disease starts out with a high fever and a hacking cough and ends with severe metabolic disturbances and nightly hallucinations. Complete recovery may take many weeks. Humans over the age of forty are more severely affected than younger ones; children rarely contract the disease.

In an infected stock of budgerigars, ornithosis affects primarily younger birds. At first one can notice the usual cold symptoms. A discharge of mucus from the beak and nasal passages is rather conspicuous, together with coughing and jerking movements of the head. Quite a common accompanying symptom is diarrhea. Young birds succumb quite quickly to this disease, while other parakeets are able to hang on for weeks and survive a bout with ornithosis. These birds are especially dangerous, since they can remain so-called latent virus carriers for months, *i.e.,* the birds excrete the virus and thus endanger other birds without being obviously sick themselves. Even just a mere suspicion of an outbreak of ornithosis should be reported to the nearest official veterinarian, something which is in the best interest of every breeder. This veterinarian is entitled to ask for, in fact he is obligated to demand, a feces sample to be examined in an institute for tropical diseases for the presence of the ornithosis virus. With modern laboratory procedures the result is available within a few days. If it is indeed positive, *i.e.,* the birds have ornithosis, the entire stock is not necessarily destroyed, provided humans have not become infected. Instead, a strict quarantine is ordered until it is shown that the disease has been eradicated. During this period birds must not be disposed of, and no outsiders are allowed to enter the breeding facility. At the same time the breeder has to give a specially prepared antibiotic-enriched feed under veterinary supervision. Budgerigars are not too fond of it and, therefore, nothing else should be given. The birds tend to lose a bit of weight and condition, but serious losses are avoided. Most of the birds can be saved using this procedure, something which, of course, is vitally important with valuable stock. The examination is repeated after a few weeks; if the result is negative, the birds are considered to be cured and are released from quarantine requirements. However, should the result still be positive, the ornithosis virus is still present and the treatment has to be repeated. This, however, rarely happens.

If birds other than budgerigars are also being kept on the same premises, these too will have to be given the antibiotic food.

Not every budgerigar disease needs to be psittacosis, but caution is always advised. A feces examination costs only a few dollars. However, any unreported cases with positive test results and with the possibility of infecting humans can cause severe difficulties and may lead to costly litigation.

Those who keep only a single bird in an indoor cage have little to worry about, since it has no contact with wild or imported birds. Modern treatment methods with corresponding medical successes have persuaded the government to loosen the import restrictions for parrots.

OTHER DISEASES

The diseases most common among budgerigars are those affecting the gastro-intestinal system, the crop and the respiratory tract. Gastro-intestinal problems can, in mild cases, be corrected in a short period of time by giving spray millet as the only food and by adequate warmth. In more persistent cases some of the broad spectrum antibiotics from the human medicine family have been very effective in proper dosages. Unfortunately, these are available only on prescription and finding the proper dosage is often problematic. One should never give more than one drop per day. Here use the same procedure as with liquid vitamins; it is imperative that the bird not be turned on its back during the treatment but instead be kept in a normal position. Most birds will recover after a treatment period of three days. In very persistent cases the treatment will have to be repeated—after an interval—for another three days. After the antibiotic has been administered the bird should also get some multi-vitamin, also given with a pipette (eye dropper) into the beak. Alternately, a drop of viscous vitamin solution can be administered from a tip of a small wooden stick held in front of the beak of the bird. The bird will instinctively snap at it and thus will take the liquid into its beak. If liquids are administered via a pipette there is—in budgerigars—an inherent danger that the liquid might go down the wrong way and the bird suffocate. An additional drop of vitamin is given after about one week. This vitamin treatment is required because antibiotics tend to kill the entire gastro-intestinal bacterial fauna. Some of these tend to utilize these required vitamins.

SOUR CROP

This disease can be very dangerous when not treated effectively and without delay. It is very prevalent during the early summer months. It is assumed that there is some connection between the occurrence of this disease and the appearance of ripened grass seeds. However, it has not been determined yet whether there is a particular pathogen involved or whether it is caused by the sudden excessive use of a natural seed which causes a fermentation process. Afflicted birds tend to empty their crops through repeated vomiting whereby they produce a sticky slime which, through violent head shaking, becomes distributed around the face, head and neck plumage.

In the final stage, the bird sits with closed eyes in a stiff and erect posture.

Strangely enough, the plumage is not fluffed up when this disease has been contracted. Instead, it appears quite smooth. The bird refuses all food and will die within 24 hours unless immediate action is taken. The antibiotic, tetracycline, has proven to be very effective. One drop given directly into the beak can often produce remarkable results within a few short hours, when the bird resumes feeding again. Rarely will the bird vomit again thereafter, and thus only one treatment is usually needed. The bird begins to clean its plumage and will bathe again, and after a few days it appears completely and totally recovered. There is, however, also a contagious crop disease which, according to KRONBERGER, directly leads to mortalities.

BRONCHIAL CATARRH AND PNEUMONIA

When treating diseases of the respiratory tract we have to distinguish between the relatively harmless bronchial catarrh and real pneumonia. Among the symptoms of both diseases are chirping or rasping breathing sounds, especially at night. The bronchial catarrh usually disappears quickly without requiring treatment; pneumonia, however, leads in many cases to death within three to eight days, providing proper counter measures have not been initiated. Usually one administers an antibiotic either as a concentrated drop given directly into the beak or, preferably, injected intramuscularly by a veterinarian. It is important for this treatment to be initiated as early as possible. In the advanced stage of this disease most birds become too weak and cannot be saved.

Once again, it has to be emphasized that in parakeets each case of pneumonia is not a case of ornithosis. Only when several birds have died under similar circumstances within a short period of time is it advisable to report this fact.

DIGESTION

The excretion of birds is an important indication of their health. Normal budgerigar droppings consist of black-white piles, which dry out quickly and which should be removed. The dark part consists of digested food and the white part is urine. Mushy or thin, yellowish feces indicate some general digestive problem; if it consists of blood one would expect a serious gastro-intestinal infection which requires immediate medical treatment. Liquid greenish feces are indicative of a gall bladder problem. In these birds one would expect a liver disorder and they should be put on an immediate rigid diet, consisting mostly of spray millet and some oatmeal. Oatmeal is a very good treatment for digestive difficulties. This food is usually eagerly taken once the budgerigars know it and if nothing else is offered.

EGG BINDING

This was a much dreaded problem among budgerigar females. However, nowadays in view of the availability of suitable vitamin products it is not considered a problem any longer. Egg binding can afflict females of any age and at any time while eggs are being produced. It is rare that the first egg produced in a young female causes this problem. Usually it is a weakened overall condition often involving deformed or shell-less eggs (which are only enclosed in a flexiblemembrane). Movement in the oviduct causes these eggs to be compressed in the middle and thus become stuck in the cloaca. At the first sign of egg binding the female will—because of increasing pain—repeatedly leave the nest box and fly, unsettled, about in the cage. Later on, she rests exhausted, fluffed up and with closed eyes on the cage bottom. She will not take any food and cannot release any feces because the egg is blocking the cloacal passage. The time has come for immediate action because otherwise the bird will die within a few hours. Often it is sufficient to keep the bird temporarily in a humid-warm environment by placing hot, wet towels around a small cage in which the bird is kept. Alternately, a handkerchief wetted thoroughly in warm water can be wrapped around the bird. This procedure tends to relieve cramps and, in most cases, the egg is discharged in a quarter of an hour or so. Another method consists of a temperature shock. Keep the female in one hand turned on its back as a short cold stream of water is directed against the cloaca. Then transfer the bird to a small cage equipped with an infra-red lamp. In most cases the egg will be released shortly thereafter. As soon as the egg has been passed the female will return to normal and begin to feed again, provided she has not been weakened through a prolonged period of egg binding. In any event, a female who has suffered egg binding should be removed from the breeding cycle until she is in prime condition again. Those eggs already laid by this bird can be transferred to other nests.

If these methods should not bring the desired effect direct manipulation becomes necessary. For that purpose the bird is held in one hand and with the index finger of the other hand, which has been lubricated with warmed vegetable oil, one massages gently the abdominal region towards the cloaca, which pushes the egg, which can be felt through the skin of the bird, gently forward. If that does not work either, one should attempt to drain the egg by piercing it with a disinfected needle inserted through the cloaca. Even that procedure does not eliminate all problems, because it is difficult to remove all the remaining egg fragments from the oviduct of the bird. Most of these fragments will be eliminated via a normal passage. Should, however, a piece with sharp edges remain, the budgerigar female will die of blood poisoning within a short period of time. Once again, however, attempt to remove shell fragments very carefully with a pair of forceps; however, such an operation on a relatively small bird requires a very steady hand and a lot of luck. Even if the egg can be successfully removed in this manner one should not have too much hope for the future of the bird. Females surviving such a procedure inevitably cannot be bred again. The operation on the delicate reproductive organs has invariably caused irreparable damage. It is, therefore, of paramount importance for the breeder to provide optimum food and care in order to avoid egg binding from the start. The process of manipulation to relieve egg-binding is almost always best left to the veterinarian.

"FRENCH MOLT" (RUNNER DISEASE)

Most budgerigar fanciers will have heard of the infamous "French Molt" or Runner Disease. It is not a disease in the conventional sense but instead a nutritional deficiency which results in the loss of the main plumage. This phenomenon has occurred since budgerigars have been bred in captivity. It appeared first in the early French hatchery operations. Hypotheses about the cause of this phenomenon and efforts to remedy it were made in the excellent literature review by STUBER. Even before that, MATERN had assumed that the loss of plumage was a nutritional deficiency resulting from insufficient amino acids which are required to produce the horny substance of the feathers. In the event that such essential nutrients are either absent or insufficient in food offered to the birds, the "French Molt" invariably occurs. A lack of amino acids can also arise when the bird rejects any protein-rich food—animal foods including egg food. Amino acid preparations and vitamin solutions are commercially available; these are added to the drinking water. Unfortunately, these substances cannot completely prevent the occurrence of "French Molt"; however, many breeders have had very good success with them. Some breeders including veterinarians tend to believe that this problem arises from virus infection.

I personally believe that there is a connection between poor grain harvests overseas in conjunction with nutritionally insufficient, poorly germinating seeds. The decisive stage in the occurrence of "runners" seems to be between the se-

The birds to the right are suffering from French molt which is often called "runner disease" because the birds cannot fly well enough to escape an enemy and they run away instead of flying away. The bird below has a feather problem because it has been plucking its own feathers. This is equally as disturbing as French molt.

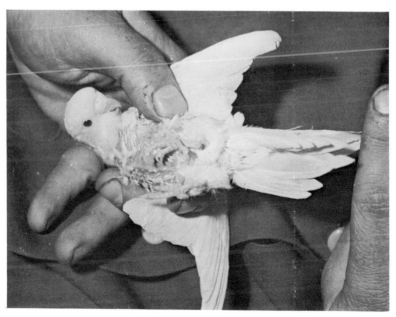

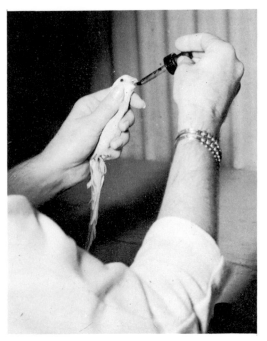

Birds with French molt disease should not be mated or even allowed to exist in the same cage with normal breeding birds as they often do mate.

cond and third week, the time of the most rapid plumage growth. If at that time the food, which still contains fore-stomach milk has an insufficient protein content, then there occurs insufficient circulation at the base of the large feathers. The wing and tail feathers will break off at the slightest touch even before they are fully grown. This occurs usually when the young are beginning to try their wings in the nest box during the fourth week, or at the latest shortly after they fly out of the box. When one takes a close look at these broken-off feathers, one invariably finds a weak cork-screw-like growth on the lower end of the blood-encrusted shaft. In the most serious cases all wing and tail feathers fall out and, thus, the deformed young birds are only able to run around at the bottom of the cage.

Apart from that these pathetic looking creatures are quite healthy and often very hardy, and they are even able to learn to climb up the wire in an aviary to reach the feed dispensers or the perches.

Some of these "runners" will re-grow their entire plumage within a few weeks; these birds are then indistinguishable from normal young budgerigars. In others, all new feather growth falls out again before the feather shafts have a chance to harden. The remaining feather stumps are continuously further damaged because of the bird's desperate attempts to fly. Eventually, the feather roots die and, with that, all hope is extinguished that such "runners" will ever become nor-mal budgerigars. They will have to be destroyed, since they are unable to lead a normal bird life. Those birds which regain their plumage should not be used for breeding, because there is a possibility that the tendency towards "French Molt" is genetically inherited.

In very severe cases of this disease even the small under-feathers fall out and totally bare patches occur. An even rarer phenomenon is the sudden case of "French Molt" in the case of well-established adult breeding birds. Sometimes these birds lose only a few primary feathers out of their wings and the long medium feathers from the tail. Most of those feathers will re-grow quickly. According to AF ANEHJELM Australian researchers observed similar symptoms on various small grass parrots. According to these reports the birds flap around helplessly in hundreds in the Australian outback. It is assumed that this phenomenon occurred in conjunction with the natural available food in Australia, possibly in conjunction with a prolonged drought.

FEATHER PLUCKING

One of the most undesirable traits among parrots, including budgerigars, is their feather plucking. It cannot really be considered a "disease" in the conventional sense. So far science only knows that this is a self-destructive, disliked habit among some birds. The exact cause is unknown. If occuring among individually-kept birds one often expects boredom to be the reason. Parrots prefer to pluck those feathers where the shafts are still filled with blood, in other words, those which are still in the process of development. This gives them a taste for fresh blood, something of which they can only be broken with great difficulty. This is—for a herbivorous bird—strictly an intuitive assumption, especially since the birds doing these self-inflicted injuries often cry out in pain. There is a spray remedy which is alleged to help in many cases, simply because it tastes and smells badly. Extensive personal involvement with the bird and fresh branches to chew on are some of the most natural and effective counter-measures.

It occurs rather rarely that nestlings are plucked of their feathers by the adult birds, something which can have rather serious consequences. The females are more inclined to do that than the males; however, both sexes have been observed doing this. This behavior is noticed by the screaming cries of the nestlings. At first the adults will systematically pluck out all down feathers, and some adult birds will stop at that. This is not too serious since the down tends to grow rapidly again and will be re-established by the time the young are ready to leave the nest. However, if the adult birds, particularly the females, also pluck primary feathers then, inevitably, large visible slow healing barren patches occur. The young birds thus afflicted will remain behind in their normal development.

If at that time the breeder does not take any measures, young birds which have only their primary feathers and a few feathers on the head will leave the nest (wing and tail feathers are usually left intact by the feather plucking adults). However, these unfortunate youngsters cannot fly properly because some of their plumage is missing. They are particularly shy, catch cold easily and require several months until their entire plumage re-grows. Once "feather pluckers" have been discovered immediate counter-measures are required. The best one is the removal of the youngsters and raising by foster parents. If the brood is not too large it may be sufficient to remove the offending parent and leave the youngsters in the care of the other. Even on bloody bare spots feathers will re-grow quickly if the youngsters are being fed well and the plucking is stopped. Incidentally, these feather plucking parent birds feed their youngsters as efficiently as they pluck their feathers. It has been shown that the tendency for feather plucking of the young is genetically controlled and is passed on from mothers to daughters. Offspring of such birds should, therefore, not be used for breeding, particularly not the females.

SCALY LEG MITES

The most dreaded parasite which occurs from time to time in budgerigar hatcheries is the scaly leg mite. Related forms of this parasite cause related symptoms in chickens and fur-bearing animals. In budgerigars this mite attacks all featherless areas, becoming initially established in the corners of the beak. Initially, it can be seen only by a trained observer; the feathers around the beak become slightly raised. Upon close examination one finds initially small, wart-like growths which rapidly increase in size until they cover the entire beak, chin area and nasal fold. Also often afflicted are legs and feet, the eyelids and the area around the anal opening. Through cleaning and scratching, the bird itself transfers the barely visible mite to other parts of its body. The parasites dig deep into the skin and cause a severe itching irritation. The growth consists of dead skin, caused through tissue changes because of the presence of the mites. In advanced stages, the entire beak degenerates. It will become brittle, small holes appear and the ends become abnormally elongated. The birds will lose weight and condition because of the constant irritation. Eventually, they will starve to death because they cannot take in sufficient food with their defective beak. This process can extend over months. At the beginning budgerigars thus afflicted show very little discomfort. This is regrettable because it is only at this stage that an effective treatment can be instituted. There is little hope for birds once the final stage has been reached.

Commercial acaricides are available, but they must be applied very carefully with a finely pointed brush onto the affected areas. One has to be particularly careful when it is applied to eyelids that the medication does not get into the eyes directly. Yet, regardless of how this medication is applied, the bird will show some discomfort. As long as the corners of the beak are the only affected areas, usually only one treatment is necessary, which can be repeated in about eight days to be quite sure that the problem has been solved. At that time one usually notices that the warts have already disappeared. In more severe cases a repeated treatment at eight-day intervals is necessary. Strangely enough not all budgerigars will be attacked by the scaly mite, not even in a crowded aviary. Nevertheless, all afflicted birds must be isolated for treatment and should not be used for breeding. Aviaries with this disease must be disinfected.

DOUBLE EGGS AND HATCHING DIFFICULTIES

An anomaly which occurs, particularly among females of the British race, is *double eggs*. These eggs contain two yolks and possibly also two germ discs. For a long time this was only known to occur among chickens. In the course of domestication this phenomenon began to occur among budgerigar females also. These eggs can immediately be spotted by their size; they are nearly twice as large as normal eggs. Strangely enough although these eggs are often fertilized, nestlings rarely hatch from them. In the course of 130 years of parakeet breeding only four cases have been publicized where viable twins have hatched and grown up. Most of the embryos die at an early stage or are so handicapped while hatching that they become stuck and suffocate. It is very difficult for the breeder to give any aid to the hatching of such eggs. It is different with single embryos which cannot leave the egg. This can be helped when one waits for exactly the right time. The vocalizing of a healthy embryo can already be heard from the seventeenth day of incubation onward. On the eighteenth day the egg shell will be at least cracked. However, when, at the end of the eighteenth day, at the blunt end of the egg a series of tiny fractures are visible, this is a sign that the embryo needs help. To provide this, one elevates the cracked shell fragments with the blunt end of a sewing needle. One has to be extremely cautious not to penetrate too deeply into the egg; if blood should appear the embryo is usually lost. If the egg skin sticks to the embryo this can be moistened carefully and be manually removed. If the embryo is still strong it will participate in its release by pushing through underneath. In many cases the embryo is able to get out of the egg shell on its own. If not, one gives the embryo further room by removing additional pieces of egg shell. This way the embryo can move head, neck and legs. Such a half-opened egg is then placed carefully under the female again. If the young bird continues to chirp strongly, the battle is usually won. Within a few hours this youngster will be able to get out of the entire shell and be fed by the female. I have seen one case where a halfway-hatched nestling has been fed by the female. This bird was unable to get out of the egg shell completely and finally died still surrounded by half of the egg shell.

Care and Training
of House Pets

According to the latest statistics, there are at least five million budgerigars being kept as house pets in the Federal Republic of Germany.

Before one or several young budgerigars are purchased as pets, the proper cage and related equipment, as well as food and sand, should be on hand. The newly arrived birds should be made to feel comfortable as quickly as possible. When an individual bird is kept, one has to remember that this is the first time that it has been separated from its parents and siblings. Moreover, the transport and the totally new surroundings will, no doubt, frighten the bird. However, individual reactions can vary substantially. One bird may "mope around" for days, while others may be extremely active, climbing around the cage, making somersaults on the wire and doing other strange contortions. None of the activities are a sign of having "settled in"; however, they diminish as the bird begins to feel at ease in its new surroundings. It is better that it be left alone as much as possible during this critical period of adjustment. Therefore, one should not attempt to take it out of the cage for the first eight to fourteen days. While being in its cage, the bird should gradually become accustomed to the new surroundings. All work on and around the cage must be done calmly and cautiously, while talking quietly to the bird. What is said to the

151

bird is irrelevant, yet this first vocal contact between owner and his pet is very important for the bird becoming tame. If the bird reacts favorably it will sit calmly and appear to listen to the voice, closing and opening its eyes. Once this stage has been reached, the cage door is slowly opened and the back of a hand pressed gently against the chest of the bird, so that it is eventually forced to climb onto the hand. The bird perceives the warmth of the human hand against its feet as pleasant, and soon it will begin to nibble on the fingers. Then the hand is cautiously pulled out of the cage, with most young birds calmly remaining on it. The budgerigar is now more familiar with the human hand than with the surrounding room furniture and the unexpected open space. It will take some time for it to embark on its first flight. After several landing failures it will finally land on some elevated location, *e.g.,* curtain rod, etc. It is imperative that the fancier not panic and go after the bird with a broom or some other object. Such a recapture attempt could spoil everything and the bird would lose its newly gained confidence. Instead, it should be left alone for some hours, until it gets hungry. Meanwhile, the bird will have realized that its cage affords protection and offers food, and that the human is a harmless companion. Soon the bird will return on its own to the cage or its keeper.

When this occurs the above procedure is repeated; the bird is taken onto the hand again and carefully returned to its cage. It will start to feed immediately and the cage door can be closed without haste; and so, the first critical round in the process of adjustment and training has been won. If the young budgerigar does not dare to come down from its landing spot, one can take the feed container and hold it in front of the bird. It is unlikely that the bird can resist such temptation. In any event, we must never be persuaded to set up another food container outside the cage; otherwise the bird will never be conditioned to consider the cage to be home and as the only place where it can find food.

Prior to the next excursion the cage door is simply opened and the bird will come out on its own and welcome the keeper. After some climbing antics on the head and shoulder of the keeper, the bird will set out on exploratory flights through the room. There are, of course, those birds which learn rapidly and those which are shy and slow to learn. The latter have to be given more attention and the keeper has to be more patient with them. Initially, all those objects which can involve the bird in accidents have to either be removed or protected, *e.g.,* windows without curtains, unprotected hot stoves and open burners; open, deep water containers and, of course, most of all open windows. The multitude of "accident" opportunities which an inexperienced budgerigar can encounter is simply incredible. Particularly dangerous are fish tanks, because the green water plants tend to entice the bird to bathe. Many birds have sunk beneath the deceiving surface cover of aquatic plants and drowned. Poisonous indoor plant leaves have to be kept away from free-flying budgerigars, since the curious birds have a tendency to chew on them.

Far less problematic is an experienced cage bird, yet it always takes a few weeks until this stage is reached. By then the bird has established its regular landing and sitting places in the room, and at each of these sites some paper or washable plastic sheets is placed down to protect against bird droppings. The feces of healthy budgerigars do not stain room furniture; after it has dried it can simply be brushed off or wiped away. If the cage has been positioned correctly, the bird will spend most of its time on the cage roof anyway, especially when there is attached a climbing branch or at least a landing perch.

Yet, with free-flying budgerigars in a room, one has to expect the occasional accident, despite all precaution. Leg and wing fractures often heal within fourteen days without requiring veterinary treatment, provided the bird is kept quiet and confined to a cage. More difficult fractures will have to

153

be splinted. For that purpose one can use two small pieces of wood, *e.g.,* flattened matchsticks. Inexperienced keepers should seek professional help from a veterinarian or at least from an experienced breeder. If the splints have been secured too tightly the blood circulation to that particular part becomes restricted, and the foot can possibly die off. Regrettably, this is also the case when a leg bone has been shattered and penetrates the skin. A rapid amputation here is the best solution. Wing fractures are best left alone. A bandage cannot be secured properly and most birds will rid themselves of it quickly. Most wing fractures will heal on their own. The worst thing that can happen is a slight dislocation of the wing position, yet this is little more than a minor beauty defect which has no adverse effect on a cage bird.

A window left open has been the fate of many tame budgerigars. An initial curiosity rapidly turns into a panic flight, when the unfamiliar air draft passes by the bird or when the traffic noise frightens it. The bird then flies blindly into the wide open space, over roofs and entire city blocks. Regardless of how tame such a bird once was, it rarely ever finds its way home again. With some luck it may become attracted by the calls from budgerigars kept in an aviary nearby, where it can then easily be caught. A similar rescue is possible when—by some remote chance—the bird flies through another open window into a room where another tame budgerigar is kept. On the basis of the leg band number, such a bird can then be returned to its owner via a Lost and Found office or an advertisement in a local newspaper.

One of the first things which should be taught to a tame pet budgerigar is the name and address of its owner. This sound mimicry has enabled many pets to be returned to their rightful owner.

Well looked-after and properly cared-for pet budgies can live surprisingly long. However, the period from the fifth to the seventh year is very critical for birds kept individually. At that stage many develop tumor-like growths on their chest, which distort their appearance and restrict their activities. As long as these growths are getting larger, they cause some pain to the birds. Later on, they will dry up and eventually fall off. Alternately, they can also be carefully removed without injuring the bird.

Malignant, cancerous tumors are more prevalent on other parts of the body, such as on neck and abdomen. Only very few veterinarians have the skill and steady hand to successfully remove tumors in such delicate locations. Aging female budgies sometimes develop abdominal dropsy, which is recognizable by a distinctly swollen abdomen, which feels spongy to touch or pressure. Regrettably, these birds cannot be saved, just as those birds which suffer from an advanced case of egg binding. The pelvis in these specimens has become too rigid to permit the passage of an egg. The formation of eggs in individually-kept females is often promoted by sugar and protein-rich foods from the human dinner table. In contrast to aviary birds, tame free-flying birds will eat most anything off the table. As long as the birds are young such an unnatural diet does little harm, provided they are kept away from spicy foods. However, for older birds from their fifth year on too much sugar, fat and protein is detrimental. The males become too fat; they age prematurely and die early. The females are stimulated to produce eggs at a stage in their lives when their reproductive capacity is beginning to decline. Fortunately, not all of these will become egg-bound. In fact, many will produce a full clutch and incubate it on the bottom of the cage. It is advisable to leave these birds alone, because after eight to fourteen days they will become discouraged and give up. Usually there are no further breeding attempts. It is, of course, far better to prevent the production of eggs through proper dietary control. Without the stimulus of a male's presence and in the absence of a nest box, such females usually do not lay eggs.

Individually kept males sometimes display their reproductive instincts through occasional regurgitation of food. This is essentially harmless and it certainly is not a disease symptom, although such activity does not look particularly attractive. Even this activity can be limited through a proper diet. Oatmeal is certainly to be avoided when individually kept budgerigars display breeding behavior. At that stage both sexes tend to masturbate occasionally, which is not detrimental to them and is only a periodic phenomenon.

At this stage, I would like to point out one danger I see in the use of a particular toy with which nearly every budgerigar cage is equipped . . . a mirror. I personally am against the use of such a toy. It, indeed, consoles a solitary budgerigar during his hours of loneliness. The bird talks to it, kisses it and even tries to feed the imaginary partner in the mirror, which tends to act, at times, as a strong sexual stimulant. Feeding the mirror image has little esthetic appeal for sensitive people, because the mirror can become unsightly.

ONE OR MORE BUDGERIGARS?

As was pointed out above, keeping solitary birds has some distinct disadvantages. Yet, the main benefit is, of course, that these birds become very tame and imprinted upon humans. Someone with less time available, yet still wanting to enjoy the company of colorful budgerigars, should keep a pair or even several in a suitably large cage. Of course, these birds will never become quite as tame as those individually kept. They are essentially preoccupied with the company of each other, and humans are considered to be little more than food providers, to whom the birds may develop a degree of friendship.

With some effort it is also possible to keep several tame budgerigars together, as the entertaining account by SWIFT indicates: He first owned a very young male, which he managed to tame and which befriended him. It was also a very talented "talker." Instead of a mirror he added to the same cage a very young, four to five month old female, which was not fully weaned yet. Pleased with such a closely resembling "toy", the young male immediately took over the father role. At that age he was not yet fully imprinted upon humans, and his feeding instinct had been stimulated. Thus, the female grew up in the custody of a completely tame "foster father" and became similarly accustomed to the human keeper. In fact, the female soon picked up the "repertoire" from the male, and the two birds began "talking" to each other, using human sounds and words. Pet owners must never become anthropomorphic and believe that their pets are actually "talking." Parakeets are only imitating noises and sounds they have heard, which, when used in a particular situation, give the impression that those birds have the ability of human reasoning. Nevertheless, "talking" budgies can indeed by very entertaining.

The above-mentioned male later on mated with the female, and during their courtship the male talked tenderly to the female, saying for instance "kiss me my darling" and so on. When the female was incubating its eggs, the male would fly up to the nest box entrance—as all budgerigar males do—and then, very surprisingly, he would call into the box with "come out, will you."

This tame pair raised their young and still maintained closeness with the humans.

With only a little appreciation for these birds one can train a pair to fly in and out of the cage, to land on the keeper, and to participate in normal family activities. It is, of course, important that the birds be acquired very young and that they are properly conditioned.

Anyone not wanting to breed budgerigars does not have to worry about a single pair starting to breed. All that needs to be done is to supply the correct natural food and to see that nest boxes are *not provided*.

For anyone who wants to be sure that no breeding occurs, it is best to acquire two males. These get along with each other at all times, they groom each other and occasionally they will even feed each other. At times, disturbing signs of sexual activities are also avoided with two males.

Although individually kept females make excellent pets, one must NEVER put two or more females together. Among budgerigars the female is the "stronger sex." Therefore, females are not compatible with each other, even if a male is present. Females tend to fight or argue about anything, at the feed container, about the best sitting or sleeping perch, etc. These arguments are not always as harmless as those among males; serious injuries to legs and heads are not uncommon, apart from the constant aggravating screeching noises.

It is also not recommended to keep several pairs in the same cage, if breeding is not desired. This leads, inevitably, to excessive fighting.

Either a single pair, or two or more males are most suitable for an indoor community cage. If such a cage is equipped with several large seed dispensers, the birds can even be left alone for a few days. Incidentally, birds in a community cage are never as care-dependent as single birds. If such a cage is sufficiently large, it can also remain closed for an extended period of time. The birds will keep each other occupied and thus get enough exercise.

MIMICRY AND "TALKING" ABILITY

Budgerigars, just as most other parrots, can imitate the human voice with surprising accuracy. This was discovered by accident in the 1930's. At that time a Mrs. RAGOTZI in Silesia used to take in regularly orphaned budgerigar youngsters from an adjoining commercial hatchery in order to raise them. She would feed—with much success—even fourteen-day-old nestlings a slightly boiled, warm mush, consisting of shelled millet (available from health food stores), oatmeal and milk (water on hot days). After having dipped their beaks into this mush repeatedly the youngsters would learn quickly to scoop up the thick food mixture from the tip of a spoon. Once the birds were four weeks old, the mush was gradually replaced with seeds, which were taken by the birds the same way. After five to six weeks the nestlings were fully weaned and as healthy as normally raised budgerigars. However, these hand-raised parakeets were completely tame and without fear, because they had learned to consider humans as one of them. While feeding the youngsters Mrs. RAGOTZI used to talk to them in order to establish a closer contact with the birds, a practice which is routinely followed when raising young animals. Of course, she was more than surprised when one of the birds "replied" with a few words in exactly her tone of voice. This was the discovery, in Germany, of the ability of budgies to mimic human language. Mrs. RAGOTZI continued to work with budgies, teaching them to "talk", and she finally published a fundamental book on this subject.

Later on, it was discovered that the hand-feeding procedure was not required to tame budgerigars and to teach them to "talk." Even fully weaned chicks can be trained within a relatively short period of time to imitate the human voice. However, these birds should not be older than about three months, although some six-month-old chicks can still pick up this talent. Yet, older birds will rarely become imprinted upon humans anymore.

What exactly do we have to do in order to teach our young budgerigar to "talk"?

The bird must be perfectly tame. It must approach the keeper willingly and calmly sit on his hand. Only then will it listen attentively to the human voice. This is indicated externally by opening and closing its eyes.

We start out with a few short words consisting mostly of vowels. These are repeated loudly and pronounced distinctly. It is useful to teach the bird its name first, which should be a simple word and must be repeated within short sentences. Right from the start it is important to use such

A cock budgerigar passing food to his mate. The pattern of the disturbed feathers on her breast indicates that she has been sitting on her eggs and has just left the nest.

This normal light blue budgie is a young bird.

short sentences, which must always be repeated in their entirety, so that for the human ear the anticipated parrot imitations will ultimately make sense. The next sentence should contain the name and address of the owner, provided this information is not too long and complicated.

Sometimes, it may take up to fourteen days until the young budgie begins to repeat the first few words. However, it is also possible that weeks, and even months, may pass until the first "human echo" is heard. Understanding and learning abilities vary greatly between individual birds, and a particular intelligence level cannot be guaranteed, by either the breeder or the dealer. After all, one also has to take into account the teaching capability of the human trying to teach the bird. Budgerigars seem to mimic more readily the higher pitched voices of women and children rather than deep male voices. Moreover, women have more patience and, therefore, they are often more successful.

The best time to work with birds is during the morning and evening hours. At the time of dusk, birds tend to be the most attentive. Once the first few words have been learned, others will be picked up more rapidly. In fact, once the mimicking process has set in, a budgie will retain and add to its vocabulary words which it has heard only occasionally. Therefore, it is important to repeat lessons frequently during the training process, otherwise the bird will learn only gibberish.

The parakeet undergoing training should not become diverted by extraneous things. So it is advisable to remove all "toys" and permit only brief excursion flights around the room. Feeding the so-called "talking beads" is useless. In my opinion, the *lecithin* contained in these beads puts more stress on the nerves of the more sensitive birds than is good for them. Healthy budgerigars are, by their nature, highly temperamental and need no stimulants, which have a tendency to make them nervous. Feather-plucking and other abnormal behavior may then become a consequence.

As a general rule, the younger the bird, the more rapidly and completely it will learn to "talk." Cocks learn easier than hens because the natural male vocal repertoire has a few more sounds than that of females. However, even hens can become good "talkers." Certain cock "virtuosos" are allegedly able to accumulate a vocabulary of up to 500 words; however, I have never heard such a bird myself. Hens with a much smaller vocabulary often "talk" more distinctly and clearly. It is very important that we do not train a "mumbler." It can be quite embarrassing to listen to a presumably highly trained, talking budgerigar, when it appears to be a ventriloquist rather than a clear and distinct imitator of words. In these cases it is only the keeper who understands the bird, because it was he who taught the bird its vocabulary. Moreover, an added problem is the fact that many budgerigars, which "talk up a storm" in familiar surroundings, become completely silent when a stranger is present. Anyway, a budgerigar rarely ever talks without intermingling its learned words with a variety of gurgling, twittering and sometimes croaking sounds. Only a few, highly talented birds separate their sound range into intermittent "talking" and uttering entire sentences, and alternating this with periods of twittering noises.

In the United States there are commercial "language schools" for budgerigars. Their mechanical operation consists of large batteries of single cages with opaque dividing walls. Each compartment accommodates one "student" and contains a tiny loudspeaker. At regular intervals a simple sequence of words is transmitted from a tape recording, which is automatically turned on and off. This procedure is continued until the majority of the birds have learned most, if not all, of the words. These birds are then sold as pre-trained "talkers" and a new batch of young birds is then processed. Apparently this has been done with considerable success.

Once a parakeet can talk a few sentences, the intensive training period can be terminated. From that stage on nearly

A 1975 variety of the British lutino.

Many new varieties of budgerigar are developed each year.

every tame "talker" will pick up additional words and sentences up to its third year. Quite often the bird will surprise its keeper with new words and word combinations. The existing vocabulary of many birds is firmly retained often until an advanced age. However, not all budgerigars are "talking geniuses." Despite intensive efforts some birds will only learn a few words; others may not learn anything at all.

Sometimes one can find real "specialists" among budgerigars which are able to imitate very effectively. Ornithologists call birds which mimic the sounds of other species "mockers"; there are many examples among the song birds. Budgerigars can be surprisingly good at this, and hens appear to be more talented than cocks. Once I had a tame hen which was able to mimic the complicated song of a gold finch with surprising similarity. Both birds were left alone all day. The gold finch was wild caught and initially very shy. This was probably the reason why it did not vocalize for a long time, although it was, otherwise, quite active. When I came home at night it was already asleep, and over the weekend it would make only a few calling sounds. The budgerigar hen had adjusted to the fact that I would only be around in the evening and then became very active.

I was very surprised one evening to be welcomed by the hen with a gold finch song. Because of this, I found out that the gold finch must have been busily practicing his singing. Later on, both birds would vocalize together or alternately, and often I had to look closely to see which bird was actually singing.

Budgerigars sometimes pick up calls and songs from city birds, which they can hear through open windows, such as green finches and blackbirds. "Conversations" between sparrows chirping outside and tame budgerigars are quite common, because budgies make a calling sound which resembles that of sparrows. Similarly, a budgerigar in a cage placed near a window to get some sun often receives sparrow visitors.

166

Playpens are fun for the bird and for you, but avoid the home-made variety with their thin wires and other death traps. Your pet shop can offer you a playpen for your budgie.

Budgerigars can also imitate, with surprising resemblance, squeaking doors, sounds from water pipes, ringing of door bells, barking dogs and other sounds.

These were high quality birds in 1955. Today they would hardly stand a chance in a good budgerigar show.

A 1958 ideal type bird which many breeders strive to achieve.

Selective Breeding

A wild animal can be changed to some degree through systematic selective breeding. If, for instance a sudden color change is observed in the plumage of a particular bird—bred either in captivity or in the wild—it often requires only a few generations of determined selection and specific pairing to permanently fix such color varieties in a particular stock of birds. However, such color change must involve, of course, a true mutation and thus must be genetically determined. Occasionally, color variations may occur—particularly light feather patches—which will not breed true. This then is a pathological pigmentation reduction, which is not genetically passed onto the next generation.

Shape and size are far more difficult to manipulate through specific breeding attempts. It requires many generations and very rigorous, continuous selection for particular characteristics. Even among races, which are considered to be firmly established (they are breeding true) there are still occasional setbacks. Some specific breeding objectives, such as a change in shape and size as well as a change in coloration, are not always readily compatible. Yet, this is exactly what breeders should strive for with such a colorful bird as our budgerigars. Much satisfactory and interesting work is still to be done in this area. The development of budgerigars is far from complete.

A pair of normal skyblue yellowfaces, mutation II, mother and son. The female is a lightwing with a dark tail. Both are pure turquoise show quality budgies of the late 1970's. The male has a better head, mask width and throat spot size. Photo from the original German edition.

172

The two outside birds are the same birds shown on the facing page; the center bird is a cinnamon opaline violet female of good shape and size, but her head is too shallow and her mask too narrow. The female's coloring and marking are very attractive; note the pink sheen. Photo from the original German edition.

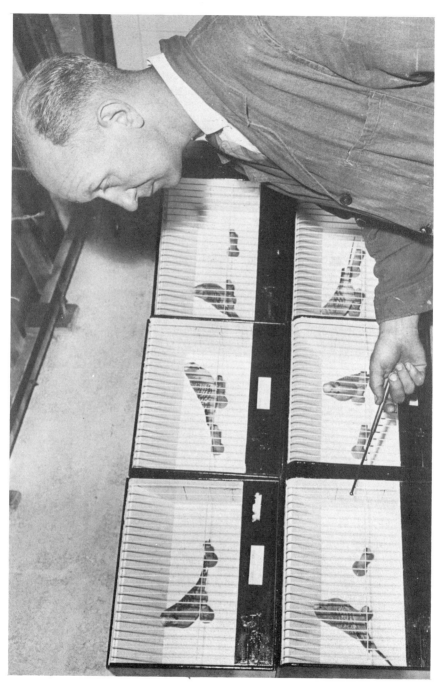

The cost of acquisition and care of a champion or show quality bird is not much more than that of an ordinary budgerigar. Visit a budgerigar show and see what the judges look for or consult the chart shown in a later section. Your pet shop can help you find a tame pet (see above) budgie if that is your goal. Or a judge (see facing page) can look for a good show specimen for you if that is your wish.

This normal lightwing, light green male has excellent wing color and truly deserves the name "yellow wing." The neck markings are too strong and the head and neck are too small. Photo from the original German text.

The bird to the left is a female royal opaline cinnamon gray without the dark factor. While she is very attractively colored and marked her forehead is curved out too far and this emphasizes her beak. The lutino female on her right is perfect in color and type, not too scrawny.

BREEDING FOR BODY SHAPE AND PLUMAGE

English breeders prefer their budgerigars to be as large as possible and, therefore, they have been breeding for decades towards this objective.

In the 1930's there was little difference between budgerigars bred in England and those in Germany. However, when, after the war, the German breeders saw the first English birds they did not believe their eyes. While the Germans were content with having been able to salvage limited stocks from the destructive war efforts to build up the trade again, the British had produced a bird with a maximum length of 21.5 cm, with a highly rounded head and a large chest, with throat dots the size of lentils.

Today we know more about the genetic details involved in producing such birds. Specific selection for size consists of continuous mating of the largest birds from a brood. The small ones are never used for breeding purposes. So, over a period involving many generations (among budgerigars one must equate one generation with one year), a certain inheritable body size becomes genetically established. However, at the same time it cannot be avoided that the plumage becomes coarse, since the individual feathers will now grow larger. The clearest evidence for this is, of course, the large throat spots, the main characteristic of today's show budgerigar. Each spot is located on an individual feather and, therefore, large spots can only be accommodated on large feathers.

Strangely enough, this phenomenon occurs even in many free-living birds. It is generally referred to as the "Yellow and Buff Theory", which is finding increasing recognition among budgie breeders. What does this mean?

For the breeding practice, "yellow" refers to an intense, shiny coloration, while "buff" describes essentially pale colors. Among canary breeders it is common to mate "yellow" birds with "buff" birds, whereby the sex is irrelevant, since this ratio is equally distributed among males and females. In

A head study of a green cock budgerigar.

A recessive pied female in yellow-face mauve, mutation I. She has good color with relatively large throat spots. Her head and wing cover markings are too dark, while those on her primary flight feathers and tail are very attractive.

An elegant albino female of the yellow type. She would make a suitable mate for a gray male, recessive in albinism and of the heavy buff type. Photos on both pages from the original German text.

A good quality British budgerigar.

international usage it is common practice to use the letter A for "yellow" and the letter B for "buff" birds. I intend to conform to this usage in this book.

"A" birds have invariably finer feathers. Each individual feather is narrower and shorter, and pigmentation is present throughout, extending into the smallest branches of each feather. This gives the overall impression that the bird is smaller and more delicate but also more color intensive. A "B" bird has plumage which is coarser and wider, and pigmentation does not extend to the outer margin of each feather. Although the basic coloration is still recognizable, the margins are distinctly paler: nearly gray in birds of dark color varieties and nearly white among the lighter colored birds. This makes such birds appear larger, but at the same time their plumage looks coarser and paler.

Among budgerigars there are, of course, also many intermediate forms, which are described as A/B birds. These transitional forms are often very difficult to separate.

Those who started the British show bird race have to be blamed for the fact that the A-B characteristic remained unrecognizable for a long period of time, or that it had not been taken into sufficient consideration. These people were only interested in birds with large spots. Thus, for years the British mated only BxB birds. The detrimental effects of this breeding, long recognized by canary breeders throughout the world, were not taken into account for a long time.

The first setback of such unnatural selective breeding soon appeared in the form of a paler base coloration, which had lost its natural sheen. Since most color varieties can only obtain a maximum of fifteen points in the show category "Color", this was not considered to be too important. Then, a new mutation appeared simultaneously in the United States and in England, with a decidedly negative characteristic, the so-called long-wing. Some of these birds had wings which were 24 cm long. They had nice heads and large spots; still, they were not attractive. The tips of their wings extended

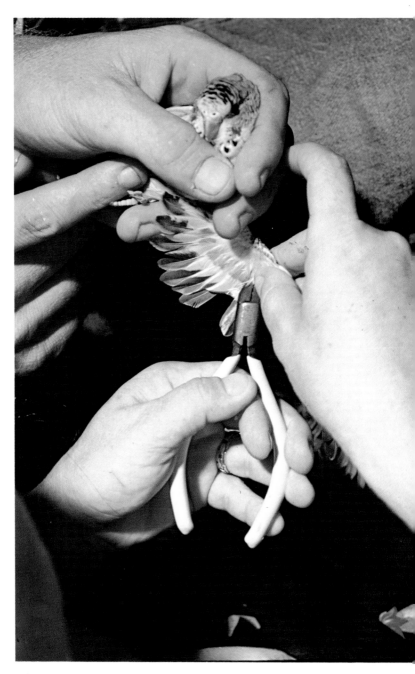

If you want to allow your budgie freedom around its cage without having it fly off, you must clip the flight feathers on one of the wings. The clipping is shown on the facing page, while the results are shown above. Photos by Dr. Herbert R. Axelrod.

beyond the upper tail feathers; the long tail was drooped downward instead of being in a straight line with the back. Since some birds appeared to have even extended backbones, they had difficulties with their center of gravity. The birds would sit crouched down on a perch, leaning forward. The long feathers appeared untidy; even worse, many birds were blind at least in one eye, some in both eyes.

All these consequences of continuous BxB matings had been known to canary breeders for a long time. Unfortunately, they are rarely familiar with both bird species. Although the heredity of long-wings proved to be dominant, these have now virtually disappeared again.

Later on, breeders paid more attention to the width of birds, by crossing long birds with shorter, more compressed ones, even with A birds. Yet BxB crosses continue to be popular, which led to the establishment of the massive, well-rounded budgerigar type of modern show standards. This, of course, could not have been done without inbreeding, which is always required for the formation of new races. Certain traits, which deviate from the norm, occur at first only in a few specimens. If such traits are to be transferred to other birds, one has to cross-breed with blood relatives, if a specific characteristic is to become permanently established. One can, therefore, assume that any highly bred race with particular true-breeding characteristics must, by necessity, be inbred. This becomes obvious from results obtained through periodically required outcrossing. If a particular race of birds has lost fertility and resistance—both negative symptoms of inbreeding—then one crosses these with one or more birds from a different blood stock. The first generation of such outcrossing is often disappointing, as far as the desired characteristics are concerned. Usually there is a more or less strong return to the original type. Yet, no successful breeder can do without such periodic outcrossing. If one is to maintain a budgerigar race of sufficiently high show standards, one often has to make two steps forward and one back.

Such a "step back" is, in this case, outcrossing with birds of a different stock or race. This does not necesarily produce birds of only inferior quality. There' are indeed different blood lines which tend to complement each other with excellent results. Yet, one has to very critically evaluate which birds from an outcrossing should be used for further breeding. This requires that all progeny be kept until they are fully grown, because birds from different blood lines often develop at different rates. Therefore, before these birds are about nine months old, one cannot really make a final judgment. At the age of six weeks some chicks may show a good shape and posture; however, after about six months they may also partially or completely stop their normal development, then all growth appears to have come to an end. On the other hand, some chicks seem to lack the desired characteristics to a point where the breeder may be tempted to dispose of them. However, there may be a few birds among them which, at some time between the fifth and the twelfth month, develop into excellent show birds. Only the very experienced eye can detect show quality in birds which do not have their adult plumage.

As far as shape and size of budgerigars is concerned, the science of genetics has still much to reveal. Nevertheless, experience has proven that shape characteristics are inherited recessively but that size is a dominant trait. Essentially this means that if a bird of a lower quality is crossed with a similar or better partner, this can indeed produce progeny of a higher quality. Therefore, one can acquire in good conscience, from a reliable breeder, young birds which are not necessarily championship material; in fact, they can even have a few flaws. If these birds are then paired off according to the advice of the breeder, they may indeed produce winning birds which are of a far superior quality than their parents. It must be remembered that an ambitious breeder will never dispose of his best birds. It took him years to produce them and only under exceptional circumstances will he part with them, of course, with commensurate remuneration.

COBALT | LIGHT YELLOW | LIGHT GREEN | SKY BLUE

GRAY | VIOLET | GRAY GREEN | LUTINO

OPALINE COBALT SELF | OPALINE BROWNWING COBALT | BLACK-EYED LUTINO | GRAYWING LIGHT GR

YELLOW-WING LT. GREEN | YELLOW-WING OLIVE GREEN | WHITEWING VIOLET | WHITEWING MA

This chart first appeared in the early 1950's.

OLIVE GREEN	MAUVE	OLIVE YELLOW	DARK GREEN
ALBINO	OPALINE DARK GREEN	OPALINE SKY BLUE	OPALINE GRAY
NNAMON SKY BLUE	CINNAMON LIGHT GREEN	CINNAMON GRAY	CINNAMON COBALT
LLOW FACE SKY BLUE	FALLOW LIGHT GREEN	WHITE or LIGHT SUFFUSION BLUE	DK.YELL.OPALINE BROWNWING

189

A beginner breeder can indeed achieve better success with a few pairs which may have some minor flaws yet are of superior extraction than if he were to buy, aimlessly, various champion birds from different stocks. However, the beginner must be cautioned against buying outright cheap birds; so-called "half-standard birds" usually have nothing to do at all with any bird standard.

Once sufficient experience has been gathered in breeding high-class budgerigars, and if sufficient space and time are available, it becomes advantageous to produce two parallel but different blood lines. Those breeders which produce the difficult recessive color varieties have to do this anyway.

What does it mean to "produce a blood line"?

We start with a cock which, according to its shape, size and plumage, is a top class bird. This bird is mated with a hen of identical qualities, irrespective of her coloration, from our own stock. For the next generation this same male is mated with one of his daughters, the hen with one of her sons; similarly the next siblings are also mated with each other. In this manner the desired hereditary traits of the original cock have been doubled, as well as those of the hen. Now all characteristics can be determined, because not only the positive ones but also the negative ones are being strengthened and will now surface. This is the disadvantage of inbreeding, something which cannot be avoided. From among the second generation only the best birds can be used for further breeding, regardless of which pair combination they are. If they are robust and healthy, a hen is mated once again with the original cock ("niece-with-grandfather combination"). After that, it is time to add new blood to this particular line.

An even better, although more difficult, method is the following: mating the highest quality cock with several hens from different blood lines during the first breeding season. In order to produce large progeny one needs the help of foster parents. The problem is that the cock has to be mated repeatedly during the breeding season, because budgerigars are, by nature, monogamous; polygamous behavior is the exception. The cock has to be taken away from the first hen before the chicks are weaned. The hen can raise two or three chicks on her own; others have to be given to foster parents. The cock is then put together with a new hen in prime breeding condition. One has to expect a transitional period of about fourteen days before the old pair-bond is broken and the cock will mate with the new hen. Since the new hen normally also requires a period of adjustment, this somewhat unnatural breeding method becomes a race with time. If the cock is to produce more progeny with additional hens during the same breeding season, it is advantageous to have him go from one to the next one as rapidly as possible. Therefore, the less he gets involved in feeding hens and chicks, the smaller is the risk of his becoming exhausted. Feeding the chicks is the most energy consuming effort for budgerigars during the breeding season.

If enough foster parents are available it may be worthwhile trying, at least once, to remove the eggs from each hen directly to another nesting pair (foster parents). However, such a method should remain the exception and not become the rule; otherwise the negative aspects of selective breeding are enhanced. Domesticated hens, which lay eggs without incubating them and rearing the chicks, should be a lesson to be observed.

If all goes according to plan, there will be a number of good to very good half-siblings at the end of the breeding season. If need be, these can be crossed further among themselves during the following year; the best daughter with the father again. The females, which in this method are not of high quality, are not used again in this blood line. Thus, the hereditary characters ("the blood", as the breeders call it) of the original (high quality) cock have been improved, which should benefit the quality of its progeny. If the stock thus established has show potential, then we have a solid basis to

The violet bird above and the green bird to the right are typical of the good quality birds now available in Germany where animal husbandry seems to take on more importance than in the Orient or in the Mediterranean countries where quantity is stressed.

A show specimen of a British budgie.

work from; subsequent generations from additional mating from among this progeny can then produce their own individual stock.

However, if genetically-produced degenerations appear, some outcrossing becomes necessary, which then must not be unduly delayed. Otherwise, there will be no further quality improvement; in fact, the entire stock may die out again very rapidly.

It is common to find, within the progeny of a particular show stock, individual chicks which barely survive, much less reproduce. Presumably, this is a consequence of continuous, exclusive BxB crosses. These unfortunate birds have abnormally elongated feathers, and primary flight feathers which are so degenerated that they cannot fly. In extreme cases the head is grossly distorted and the eyes are not visible; in fact, the birds have difficulty seeing.

Fortunately, those cases are rare exceptions; yet, unfortunately, molting difficulties and crop blockages among these highly bred birds are fairly common. Molting difficulties often occur during the changeover to adult plumage; this condition is particularly noticeable along the chest and abdomen of the birds. There, where the colors of a parakeet should be smooth and shiny, are patches of whitish down feathers. Individual cover feathers become elongated and then die off.

These remarks are not intended to destroy the ambitions or illusions of those who would like to breed top-line birds. Yet, I have to point out quite emphatically the inevitable necessity to include the "A" birds in selective breeding work.

Crop blockages, due to air being swallowed, have so far been observed only in certain doves bred specifically for this characteristic. Some stocks of British show budgerigars now have a tendency toward this same problem. The result is not particularly attractive. During the courting period, the crop of such an afflicted cock becomes so enormously swollen that, when the bird bows in front of the hen, the feathers will stand on their ends and the naked skin can be seen shining through. Such a bird, with its courting mood suddenly waned, looks absolutely pathetic—as if it has swallowed a giant dumpling. Very gradually, and only when the bird is left alone, will the air escape from the crop again. This phenomenon does not appear in show cages, since a solitary bird is not being stimulated into courting behavior. Females sometimes also have this same affliction.

BREEDING FOR COLORS

It is customary to talk about color standards rather than color varieties for budgerigars. There are only very few color mutations where color standards were developed through combination and selective breeding. The multitude of colors and color combinations may be confusing for the beginner, so that he has to look at the development of these in order to understand them better.

All budgerigar colors can be divided up into two main categories: the green series and the blue series. The birds in the green series resemble, roughly speaking, the coloration of the original Australian wild form. The birds in the blue series were developed through a mutation-loss of yellow color pigments.

All colors have been developed in this manner during the last 130 years of parakeet breeding. Invariably, they appeared suddenly in individual birds and from there they were maintained through systematic selective breeding. The same holds true for the coloration of markings, which range from black to gray and brown to white (white occurs due to the complete absence of color pigments).

The primary breeding objective of some breeders is production of birds of the English race, while others see their ultimate goal in breeding attractive colors and color combinations. There should really not be such strict separation between these goals. It is a well-known fact that some genetically-dominant color varieties can be improved more easily as a type than others. Genetically-recessive color varieties are far more difficult to work with in that respect. Invariably, the more difficult ones are also the more attractive, as far as colors are concerned. These could even be further improved yet, if breeders would attempt to breed for type and size also. Therefore, one can categorize budgerigar breeding into those who work with show budgerigars and those who produce tame birds for the trade. Many breeders are involved in both of these.

If breeding is to be for particular colors, one follows essentially the same pathway as described for the production of shape. However, it is far easier to breed for colors since the genetics are well known and predictable. The basic rule is that the greens and blues cancel each other. Crossing blue birds with those from the green series, or the other way around, produces color intensity. The most beautiful green and blue parakeets are produced from crossing blue/green x blue. We find a similar reciprocity for the mask and size of the throat spots by crossing parakeets with normal colors with opaline birds. When crossing normal birds with cinnamon-colored ones, we get a thickened plumage and a deep base coloration as reciprocal effects. Further examples will be given when the different colors are discussed in detail.

The British Show Budgerigar— Standards of the Ideal Budgerigar

So far, much has been said about the British breed of budgerigar; it is about time now for it to be formally introduced. At this stage, it has to be pointed out that the set standard never is and, in fact, never can be reached. If indeed it could be obtained, then all incentives for perfection would be lost to the breeders. That was exactly what happened in England during the mid-1960's. Therefore, in 1969 the British decided to change the standards. The German clubs had to follow, although the majority of breeders still had difficulties in even approaching the precious ideal standard. Here now is the 1970 revised internationally accepted standard for budgerigars. It requires that the head be larger, the chest and shoulder width be fuller, and the mask to feature even larger throat spots. In Germany, the more recent Federal and State exhibitions have shown, in all classes, that show birds are now being bred which come close to the new ideal standard.

In order to give beginners an easier start the DWV (German Budgerigar Breeding Club) has introduced achievement categories based upon the British system. In England the exhibitors are divided into four categories. These are the "beginners", the "breeders", the "advanced" and the "champions." The latter is the highest achievement category with the strongest competition. If a particular level of achievement is not reached each year, an exhibitor will be dropped from that category. All beginners start out at the bottom. They advance to the "breeders" as soon as they get three class winners in major show classes from at least seven birds exhibited. Alternately, a beginner must have won five medals in State or Federal shows. After similar achievements as a "breeder", an advancement to the "advanced" category is possible. Demotion from these categories is not possible. The exhibitors compete only within each category for class winners, for group winners in all color varieties, as well as for State and Federal winners. However, at State and Federal exhibitions all exhibitors compete jointly, so that each has equal chances to win the highest awards for his birds.

CHARACTERISTICS OF THE
IDEAL SHOW PARAKEET

(The following is taken from the AZ-DKB unified standard; AZ = Exchange Center of the Exotic Bird Fanciers and Breeders, Germany—reg. location Munich; DKB = German Canary Breeder Association. Published with permission granted by AZ.)

Condition: Essential. If a bird is not in condition it should never be considered for any award.

Type: Strong and thickset body shapes predominantly harmoniously rounded. Shoulder and neck wide. With a straight back line, body from nape to tip of tail gently tapered. Chest rather deep and nicely curved. The entire bird should appear compact and heavy, without being fat.

Length: About 21.5 cm from the crown of the head to the tip of tail.

Wings: Approximately 2/5 the total length of the bird, well braced, carried just above the cushion of the tail and not crossed. The ideal length of the wing is 9.5 cm from the butt to the tip of the longest primary flight feathers, which must contain seven visual primary flight feathers fully grown and not broken.

Tail: In continuation of the body axis, carried straight, feathers smooth and tight, arranged in pairs and fully grown (including the two longest feathers).

Position: Steady on a perch at an angle of 60° from the horizontal, looking fearless and natural. Body must not touch the perch.

Head: Large, round, wide and symmetrical, when viewed from every direction; curvature of skull commencing at cere, to lift outward and upward, continuing over the top and to base of head in graceful sweep.

Beak: Small and set well into face; upper beak to extend over the lower beak.

Eyes: To be bold and bright, and positioned equal distance from front, top, and back skull.

Neck: To be short and wide when viewed from either side or front.

Color: According to relevant standard, clean and evenly distributed without extraneous discoloration.

Mask and Throat Spots: To be clear, deep and wide, extending from top of head to below the throat and toward the chest, and where demanded by the standard should be ornamented by six evenly spaced large round throat spots, in the lower third of the mask, evenly spaced, forming a complete neck chain, the outer two being partially covered at the base by cheek patches, the size of the spots to be in proportion to the rest of the make-up of the bird. Coloration of mask, throat spots and cheek patches according to the respective standard requirements.

Legs and Feet: Legs should be straight and strong, two front and two rear toes and claws firmly gripping perch. Coloration according to respective standard requirements.

Markings: According to standard requirements for the various color varieties, *i.e.,* either standing out clearly and distinctly, well defined, as ghost markings only, or completely absent.

The standard guidelines listed above (characteristics of the ideal show budgerigar) are maximum requirements. Deviations from these are counted as demerits. In Germany, these were formerly counted on a score card as minus points, *i.e.,* a point system was used to judge parakeets. Since 1970 the British placing system has been used in larger State and Federal shows and in so-called "open shows", open to all participants from all Federal states. (The British Placing System: Placing in the sequence from 1 to 7 within each class, with the show cages marked accordingly. This is followed by judging of all class winners for best of show.) In small local shows the marking system is commonly used, an interim solution between the point and placing systems. In addition, there is the class X (= open) for all four exhibitor categories; this is to be used for newly purchased or exchanged birds with leg bands from previous owners, in order to assess their value. All other classes are only for a breeder's own stock; the closed leg band with the membership number is evidence of proper ownership.

MISTAKES AND GUIDELINES FOR THE EVALUATION OF SHOW BUDGERIGARS

Show Condition: As mentioned above, this is absolutely essential. Basically it refers to the overall health of the bird, the condition of its plumage, as well as its deportment on the perch in a show cage. The latter depends upon the extent of its training. If these characteristics, which are essential for a show bird, leave much to be desired, such a budgerigar should be excluded from further consideration in the show. Relevant remarks are to be entered on the score card. This should include constant fluffing up of the plumage, sleeping on both legs, excessively fat or projecting breast bone (excessive weight loss), caked and encrusted feathers around anal opening, strongly bleeding wounds, more than two throat spots missing (except varieties which do not have this feature), bloodied feather stalks, bare patches and the least indication of any pathogenic plumage or skin disorder. This applies also to those birds which have damaged their plumage through continuous fluttering around in their cage and which will not settle, even for a few seconds, on the perch provided. Minor condition flaws involve the deduction of at least two points, depending upon the nature of the demerit and what criteria are affected, *i.e.,* type, position, color, markings, etc. Birds not yet in adult plumage are to be excluded.

Type: As mentioned above, the type has been changed to favor a wide, robust and compact but not very elongated bird. This is particularly obvious in the shoulder and breast region, in comparison to the former long and slender type (please refer to the new standard of the ideal budgerigar). Nowadays, the desired large, wide and high head form looks only proper on broad shoulders. "Type" essentially refers to generally harmonious body proportions. All deviations should be noted; minor ones should incur the loss of at least three points, major ones ten points or more.

BUDGERIGAR EVALUATION CHART
(Reprinted with permission of the DWV, German Budgerigar Friends.)
1. Head too small and flat.
2. Growth on eyelids.
3. Beak projects, has cracks and growths.
4. Throat spots are irregular and too close to each other.
5. Mask is poorly delineated.
6. Neck is concave.
7. Chest is too flat.
8. Abdomen too full and feathers ruffled.
9. Wing is too long and one primary is missing.
10. Tail covert is not smooth.
11. Tail is damaged.
12. Hanging tail.
13. Growth on foot.
14. Missing claw.

SCHEMATIC DRAWINGS
These drawings deal with the posture of a bird with a bad leaning position, crossed long wings and a full abdomen.
A. Posture too steep and straight.
B . Resting bird with sagging abdomen and "knapsack" tail covert.
C . Concave back and long wing.
D . Full neck and too fat.

Length (Size): In the majority of all show budgerigars this criterion leaves hardly anything to be desired. Dimensions below standard, as far as length, width and body volume are concerned, should be penalized with at least five points, obviously stunted growth with ten points. These guidelines apply to dimensions above as well as below standard.

Wings (including position of wings): Budgerigars with obviously crossed wings will rarely ever make good show birds. Crossed wings, as a symptom of nervousness, should be assessed with two minus points. "Long wings" (mutation), where the tips of the primaries extend beyond the upper tail coverts, can usually be recognized by wings kept too low and by a hanging tail. Such deviations should be penalized with at least five to ten points, for missing feathers two points each, for damaged feathers (condition) at least three points total; similar for strongly hanging wings or for wings held too high on the body.

Tail: One has to look for damage, bent or spreading feathers, as well as for tails which are too long. The latter are invariably noticeable by "drooping" just below the body axis. Two to five demerit points should be given depending upon the extent of the faults. A missing, long tail feather should be penalized with the deduction of five points.

Position: Good show birds are not only in good condition, but they are also well-trained and thus rarely have poor deportment. An unsatisfactory position is often caused by fear, and an experienced judge will have to make the necessary adjustment. Permanent faults are a concave or convex back, a leg position deviating from the norm or a backbone which is too long (see "long wings"); condition faults, insufficient breast musculature or more commonly a heavy, fat body, virtually laying on the perch. Penalties should be minimally five points or higher. The desired deep and nicely curved chest must not be confused with a layer of fat. Therefore, the angle of the bird in relationship to the perch is smaller in heavier birds. However, as soon as these birds go into their show or courting position this angle will increase again. Here only a judge who is a breeder himself can make the correct determination. Thus an older hen with a larger abdomen, which may touch the perch, should lose fewer points than a young cock with the same fault.

Head: This is without doubt the most important characteristic of any show budgerigar. It is very difficult to breed for this characteristic and to obtain the desired size and shape, and to keep it "in line." Show budgerigars which have good heads have already won half the battle. Yet, many show birds are still lacking in suitable head-width and depth (when viewed from above) and in a properly curved forehead. For the small head of the common budgerigar with its projecting beak, despite its otherwise quite possible attractive coloration, the penalty should be twelve points; eight points for small but reasonably well proportioned heads. Significant faults include narrow or flat heads, as well as a falling or bulging nape. Each of these faults requires the deduction of five points. A proper show budgerigar head starts at fifteen points. Hens are permitted to have a flatter forehead with still broader curved sides. So called "roosterheads" in hens are not considered to be faults.

Beak: projecting as well as high-set beaks are common faults. Other faults: cracks and scrapes, injuries, deformities of the cere (including color deviations from the norm). Penalty is two to five points. Upper beak resting inside lower beak is a genetic deformity; such a bird has to be disqualified.

Eyes: Birds with eye problems, including inflamed eye lids, are to be excluded from participation. Attention has to be paid to correct position and color of the eyes (as per relevant

Be wary of buying your pet budgie from a colony such as this one. Birds raised this way usually have such a mixed background that you won't be able to breed them with any assurance of their genetic makeup. Colony birds usually are more difficult to tame and train, too.

standard description). Two or more penalty points for discrepancies.

Neck: A commonly observed fault is a narrow, constricted neck—up to five penalty points (see also the standard requirements for the head).

Color: To be in accordance with relevant standard descriptions. Olive green, mauve, lutinos, albinos, lightwings and violet birds appear to have most of the commonly observed color deviations; gray-green, gray and light black-eyes have the least problems. Because of the commonly occurring incrossing of the violet factor into dark green and dark blue birds, there appears to be some variation in the color tone from one bird to the next. This is permissible between individual birds but not on the same bird. The correct assessment of colors requires not only a keen eye but also a thorough understanding of the origin and development of colors and the effect of changing light situations upon different colors. Because of increasing show participation, together with a lack of suitable show facilities, a judge has to be able to correctly determine colors, even under artificial light. Thus, it has to be remembered that yellow lighting highlights the birds of the green series and reduces the color intensity among the blue series. Fluorescent lights have a reverse effect. Most light sources of neutral white are the most useful; however, they absorb the yellow from yellowfaces. Subdued daylight (dusk and dawn) pushes blue to violet and violet to lilac. Apart from variable shades on the same bird, the more serious faults which can be encountered among birds with dark colors are light patches due to flaws in plumage. These are, of course, condition deficiencies, which have to be assessed accordingly. Other problems are: lutinos which are too pale or which have a greenish sheen; albinos with a bluish sheen; lacewings with lack of contrast; continental pied and opaline with washed out, pale colors;

208

mutation I, yellow face, with too much yellow. In order to be able to make the necessary point adjustments, both exhibitors and judges have to be thoroughly familiar with the point scale. For colors, this scale ranges from ten to 35 points, and demerits are to be assessed accordingly. Therefore, a crest with a maximum of ten color points can only be assessed four to five minus points for pale coloration. However, a lutino, with a maximum of 35 points, can possibly be assessed fifteen to seventeen minus points. On the average, birds with a maximum of fifteen points should not be penalized more than five to seven points. Yet, deduction for inferior colors should not be made routinely or for the sake of convenience, if indeed a maximum score appears justified. Yet, a pied or normal budgerigar, which has difficulties achieving full compliance for throat spots, will invariably find it easier to get the full score for color than a lutino, albino or lacewing. Although the point scale attempts to be just and fair to all, this goal can only be achieved with care and responsibility in applying the various color standards.

Mask and Throat Spots: Split masks, simultaneously with unevenly spaced throat spots and small and narrow masks which cannot accommodate all spots satisfactorily, are the most common faults. Small and split masks are to be assessed two to five minus points, defective or missing throat spots at least one point each, whereby one has to consider the variable maximum amount of points (ten or fifteen). Wild birds have their throat spots merely indicated as lines; in common budgerigars throat spots are small, teardrop-like, yet show parakeets should have spots as large and round as possible. Spots of different sizes and arrangement are the most common faults (not in line or unevenly spaced). Otherwise, good birds often have double chains of spots running into each other. The removal of extra spots is permitted, as long as this does not affect the overall appearance of mask

Harry V. Lacey, England's foremost bird photographer presents these two portraits (see facing page also) of show quality British budgies. Note the beautiful round throat spots of the bird on the facing page.

211

and spots. If improper "trimming" causes gaps in the plumage, this is to receive at least two minus points. The elongated cheek spots are usually flawless in most color varieties. A judge has to look for typical coloration as per prescribed standards. A spotted or otherwise imperfect forehead has to be included in an assessment of the mask and spots, and thus should be penalized with two to eight minus points. Masks which lack all desired characteristics have to incur a penalty of ten minus points.

Legs and Feet: Very heavy birds tend to become bow-legged and then show incorrect foot and toe positioning (toes on top of perch instead of grasping around it). This promotes uneven and repeatedly curved, long nails, the so-called "corkscrews." Birds with this problem can easily be recognized by their incorrect, tight body position. Since feet and leg faults—whether these be hereditary or pathogenic—are part of a bird's condition, at least five points will have to be deducted for that; similarly for a missing claw. Two missing claws or generally crippled legs, feet or claws eliminate the birds from competing. Leg color has to be assessed according to the particular color standard.

Markings: All deviations from the standard, such as thinned-out or washed out designs, undesired increases and incorrect arrangements are to be penalized relative to the respective color standard (one to seven minus points). Since most color varieties only give five points for markings, deductions can, of course, be only in the range of one to three points. Most normal birds in good plumage have a few minor imperfections in their markings. Opalization is a common flaw, which should be penalized with no more than three minus points, similarly for markings which are too dark, especially on cinnamon cocks. The body coloration of opaline birds is part of the color standard, thus a special assessment for markings (maximum fifteen points) can only be made for recessive pieds. Under these circumstances three to five points may be deducted per individual fault.

Pairs: The objective of this category is to select pairs well balanced as far as coloration and markings are concerned, so that the best can be shown in open competition. The judge proceeds at first as if only one bird is to be judged, considering that only 35 points are available in the first position. The accumulated penalty points from all other positions are then being deducted for cocks and hens, and the resultant totals are added and then divided by two. Quality differentials for cocks and hens are rounded off upward (by small differentials) or downward (large differentials). The remaining points are then awarded for compatibility of the pair. The highest marks are to be given to those pairs where the individual birds are as identical as possible, in as many desirable traits as possible. Utilization of these ten extra points depends upon the ability and experience of the judge. Only in this manner can the judging of pairs have any merit if it is to improve breeding standards.

Collection: For the evaluation of four or six parakeets of identical markings and colors, one applies the same criteria as under "pairs." Yet, the collection has to be assessed in its entirety, so individual marks can only be used as guidelines. The cumulative value, however, is of course affected by the quality of individual birds. The ten extra points are proportioned toward the harmony of the group, special color qualities of the group or rarity of the birds exhibited, all these qualities which have to be shared uniformly among the birds exhibited. Collections of four birds should receive only a maximum of seven extra points, six birds can get the entire ten points. Because of arithmetical difficulties collections of five birds are not permitted. The sex ratio among collections should be as even as possible, such as 2,2 or 3,3. Alternately, all birds can be of the same sex such as 4,0; 6,0; 0,4 or 0,6.

However, it is preferred that collections of young birds be exhibited in a separate class. If a collection includes birds which are sick or in poor condition, the entire "collection" is to be eliminated. If, at a particular show, collections are judged by ages, young birds will have to be exhibited in their own respective class.

Deducting the aggregate penalty points from 100 provides the final score. This has to be calculated very carefully for the top three places, since four to nine different intermediate results will have to be considered. However, judges are not obligated to determine for each individual bird the specific point score. These scores are essentially only guidelines for the overall evaluation, except in international shows.

Cages: Individual birds and pairs have to be exhibited in single cages; collections in so-called collection cages.

Collection Cage: Same as a single cage, but with the follwing outer dimensions: width 514 mm, height 330 mm, depth 225 mm; sides: 219 mm x 314 mm (door 100 x 100 mm); bottom: 498 x 212 mm; lid: 514 x 194 mm; roof slope: 498 x 198 mm; facial board: 498 x 50 mm; backwall: 514 x 243 mm (thickness 6 mm); perches: length 194 mm, thickness 14 mm (diameter); regulation drinking container: half-round plastic above facial board; inside (drinking tubes not permitted); color of wire: white; cage interior: white; outside: black.

COLOR STANDARDS

Light Green—Mask: Buttercup of an even tone ornamented on each side of throat with three clearly defined black spots, one of which appears at the base of the cheek patch. Cheek patches: Violet. General Body Color: Back, rump, breast, flanks and underparts, bright grass-green of a solid and even shade throughout; markings on cheeks, back of head, neck and wings, black and well-defined on a buttercup ground. Tail: Long feathers blue-black.

Dark Green—As above but of a dark laurel-green body color. Tail: Long feathers darker in proportion.

Olive-Green—As above but of a deep olive-green body color. Tail: Long feathers darker in proportion.

Light Yellow (including Cinnamon Light Yellow)—Mask: Buttercup; back, rump, breast, flanks, wings and underparts, buttercup and as free from green suffusion as possible; primaries lighter than body. Tail: Long feathers lighter than body color.

Dark Yellow (including Cinnamon Dark Yellow)—As above but of a deeper body color.

Olive Yellow (including Cinnamon Olive Yellow)—As above but of a mustard body color.

Skyblue—Mask: Clear white ornamented on each side of throat with three clearly defined black spots, one of which appears at the base of the cheek patch. Cheek Patches: Violet. General Body Color: Back, rump, breast, flank and underparts, pure skyblue; markings on cheeks, back of head, neck and wing, black and well-defined on a white ground. Tail: Long feathers blue-black.

Cobalt—As above but body color purplish mauve, with a tendency to a pinkish tone. Tail: Long feathers darker in proportion.

Violet—As Skyblue but of a deep intense violet body color. Tail: Long feathers darker in proportion.

Whites (including Cinnamon Whites) of Light Suffusion—Mask: White. General Body Color: Back, rump, breast flanks, and underparts, white, wings and tail pure white.

NOTE—The only difference in the various varieties of white is in the cheek patches, which in every case are a pale color of the variety they represent.

Whitewings, Whites of Deep Suffusion and Cinnamon-Whites of Deep Suffusion (including Skyblue, Cobalt, Mauve, Violet and Gray)—Mask: White, ornamented on each side of the throat with three gray spots (the paler the better), one of which appears at the base of the cheek patch. General Body Color: Back, rump, breast, flanks and underparts, very heavily suffused, body color approximating to the normal variety. Wings and Tail: Pure white. Cheek Patches: In every case a pale color of the variety they represent.

Graywing Light Green—Mask: Yellow, ornamented each side of throat with three clearly defined spots of smoky gray, one of which appears at the base of the cheek patch. Cheek Patches: Pale Violet. General Body Color: Back, rump, breast, flanks, and underparts, pale grass-green. Markings on cheeks, back of head, neck and wings, should be smoky gray, half-way between black and zero. Tail: Long feathers smoky gray with pale bluish tinge.

Graywing Dark Green—As above but of a light laurel-green body color. Tail: Long feathers darker in proportion.

Graywing Olive-Green—As above but of a light olive-green body color. Tail: Long feathers darker still in proportion.

Graywing Skyblue—Mask: White, ornamented each side of throat with three clearly defined gray spots, one of which appears at the base of the cheek patch. Cheek patches: Light Violet. General Body Color: Back, rump, breast, flanks and underparts, clear pale skyblue. Markings: on cheeks, back of head, neck and wings: pure gray, halfway between black and zero. Tail: Long feathers grayish blue.

216

Graywing Cobalt—As above but of a pale cobalt body color, with tail of corresponding color.

Graywing Violet—As Graywing Skyblue, but of a pale violet body color, with tail of corresponding color.

Graywing Mauve—As above but of a pale mauve body color, with tail of corresponding color.

Graywing Gray-Green—As Graywing Light Green but with body color of light mustard-green. Cheek Patches: Light Gray. Tail: Long tail feathers deep gray.

Graywing Gray—As Graywing Skyblue but with body color of pale gray. Cheek Patches: Pale gray. Tail: Feathers deep gray.

Cinnamon Light Green—Mask: Yellow, ornamented on each side of throat with three clearly-defined cinnamon-brown spots, one of which appears at the base of the cheek patch. Cheek Patches: Violet. General Body Color: Back, rump, breast, flanks and underparts, pale grass-green. Markings on cheeks, back of head, neck, and wings: cinnamon-brown well-defined on a yellow ground. Tail: Long feathers dark blue with brown quill.

Cinnamon Dark-Green—As above but of a light laurel-green body color. Tail: Long feathers darker in proportion.

Cinnamon Olive-Green—As above but with a light olive-green body color. Tail: Long feathers darker in proportion.

Cinnamon Skyblue—Mask: White ornamented on each side of throat with three clearly defined cinnamon-brown spots, one of which appears at the base of the cheek patch. Cheek Patches: Violet. General Body Color: Back, rump, breast,

217

flanks, and underparts, pale sky-blue. Markings on cheeks, back of head, neck and wings: cinnamon brown on white ground. Tail: Long feathers blue with brown quill.

Cinnamon-Cobalt—As above but with general body color of pale cobalt. Tail: Long feathers as above but cobalt.

Cinnamon-Mauve—As above but with general body color of pale mauve. Tail: Long feathers as above but mauve.

Cinnamon-Gray—As Cinnamon Skyblue but with body color of pale gray. Tail: Long feathers of deep cinnamon shade.

Cinnamon Gray-Green—As Cinnamon Light Green but with body color of pale gray. Tail: Long tail feathers of deep cinnamon shade.

Cinnamon-Violet—As Cinnamon-Skyblue but with general body color of pale violet. Tail: Long tail feathers of pale cinnamon shade.

NOTE—In all forms of Cinnamon the male bird carries a deeper shade than the female.

Fallow Light Green—Mask: Yellow, ornamented on each side of throat with three clearly defined brown spots, one of which appears at the base of the cheek patch. Cheek Patches: Violet. General Body Color: Back, rump, breast, flanks and underparts, yellowish green. Markings on cheeks, back of head, neck and wings: dark brown on a yellow ground. Eyes: Clear red or plum. Tail: Long feathers bluish gray.

Fallow Dark Green—As above but with pale laurel-green body color. Tail: Long feathers darker in proportion.

Fallow Olive-Green—As above but with light mustard-olive

body color. Tail: Long feathers darker in proportion.

Fallow Skyblue—Mask: White, ornamented on each side of throat with three clearly defined brown spots, one of which appears at the base of the cheek patch. Cheek Patches: Violet. General Body Color: Back, rump, breast, flank and underparts, pale skyblue. Markings on cheek, back of head, neck and wings: dark brown on a white ground. Eyes: Clear red or plum. Tail: Long feathers bluish gray.

Fallow Cobalt—As above but with a warm cobalt body color. Tail: Long feathers darker in proportion.

Fallow Mauve—As above but with a pale mauve body color of pinkish tone. Tail: Long feathers darker in proportion.

Fallow Violet—As Fallow Skyblue but with a pale violet body. Tail: Long tail feathers darker in proportion.

Light Forms—The Committee recognizes the existence of a light form of Cinnamon and Fallow identical to the normal already described, but lighter in body color and markings.

Pure Yellow Red-Eyes (Lutinos)—Buttercup throughout. Eyes: Clear red. Tail: Long feathers and primaries grayish-white.

Pure White Red-Eyes (Albinos)—White throughout. Eyes: Clear red.

Yellow-Wing Light Green—Mask: Buttercup, ornamented on each side of throat with three smoky-gray spots (the paler the better), one of which appears at the base of the cheek patch. General Body Color: Back, rump, breast, flanks and underparts, bright grass-green. Wings: Buttercup. Tail: Long feathers pale grass-green.

Yellow-Wing Dark Green—As above but with general body color of laurel-green; long tail feathers darker in proportion.

Yellow-Wing Olive-Green—As above but with general body color of olive-green. Tail: Long feathers darker in proportion.

Opaline Light Green—Mask: Buttercup yellow, extending over back of head and merging into general body color at a point level with the butt of wings, where undulations should cease, thus leaving a clear "V" effect between top of wings so desirable in this variety; mask to be ornamented by six large black throat spots, the outer two being partially covered at the base of violet cheek patches. General Body Color: Mantle (including "V" area or saddle), back, rump, breast, flanks and underparts, bright grass-green. Wings: To be iridescent and of the same color as body; markings should be normal and symmetrical; long tail feathers not to be lighter than mantle.

Opaline Dark Green—As above but of a dark laurel-green body color. Tail: Long feathers darker in proportion.

Opaline Olive-Green—As above but of an olive-green body color. Tail: Long feathers darker in proportion.

Opaline Skyblue—As above but with a skyblue body color and suffusion, and white mask instead of buttercup. Tail: Long feathers not to be lighter than mantle.

Opaline Cobalt—As Skyblue but of a cobalt body color. Tail: Long feathers darker in proportion.

Opaline Mauve—As Skyblue but of a mauve body color. Tail: Long tail feathers darker in proportion.

220

The true show budgerigar should be an imposing sight.
Photo by Harry V. Lacey.

Opaline Violet—As Opaline Skyblue but of a deep intense violet body color. Tail: Long feathers not to be darker than mantle.

Opaline Gray—As Opaline Skyblue but with body color of solid gray. Tail: Long tail feathers to be not lighter than mantle; cheek patches of gray.

Opaline Gray-Green—As Opaline Light Green but with body color of dull mustard-green. Tail: Long tail feathers not to be lighter than mantle; cheek patches of gray.

Yellow-Face—Mask only: Yellow, otherwise exactly as corresponding normal variety.

NOTE—yellow-marked feathers in tail permissible.

Yellow-Face Mutation I—Same as in the above mentioned blue series but mask yellow; markings of outer tail feathers yellow.

Yellow-Face Mutation II—As above but entire plumage more or less a strong hint of yellow. This turns the light blue to turquoise, and the dark blue and violet to a deep blue-green (aquamarine), mauve to olive-gray; the wave-like markings get a pale yellow background color. The colors of dark blue, violet and mauve birds can show various shades on different parts of the body (chest, abdomen and back), but they have to harmoniously flow together.

Yellow-Face and Yellow-Head Mutation I and II in White-Blue—As in Normal, Opaline and Cinnamon-White-Blue but mask or head yellow. The entire plumage with a hint of yellow, whereby champagne colors and sea-green hues are created. Outer tail feathers with pale yellow markings.

Mutations I and II are not separated since they are very difficult to distinguish.

Yellow-Face (Albino) Mutation I and II—Cream to lemon yellow over the entire body; other than that as in Albino.

Yellow-Face and Yellow-Head (Lacewings) Mutation I and II—Same as in White Lacewings but mask and/or head yellow. Base color cream to lemon yellow; hint of yellow on markings.

Gray—Mask: White, ornamented on each side of throat with three clearly defined black spots, one of which appears at the base of the cheek patch. Cheek Patches: Gray. General Body Color: Back, rump, breast, flanks and underparts, solid gray. Markings on cheeks, back of head, neck and wings: Black and well-defined on a white ground. Tail: Long feathers black.

NOTE—The terms, Light, Medium and Dark, describe the skyblue, cobalt and mauve forms respectively.

Light Gray-Green—This variety conforms to the standard for light green except in the following details: Cheek Patches: Gray. General Body Color: Dull mustard-green. Tail: Long feathers black.

Medium Gray-Green—This term denotes the dark green form of the gray.

Dark Gray-Green—This form represents the gray olive-green.

Slate—Mask: White, ornamented on each side of throat with three clearly defined black spots, one of which appears at the base of the cheek patch. Cheek Patches: Violet. General

Closeup of a bird that would have been truly outstanding in the 1960's but would be common in the 1980's. Harry V. Lacey photo.

Body Color: Back, rump, breast, flanks and underparts, even greenish slate. Markings on cheeks, back of head, neck and wing: Black and well defined on a white ground. Tail: Long feathers blue-black.

NOTE—The terms Light, Medium and Dark, describe the skyblue, cobalt and mauve forms respectively.

Light Slate-Green—In every respect as the standard for light green, except that the general body color is sage-green.

NOTE—The terms Light, Medium and Dark describe the light green, dark green and olive forms respectively.

Crests (general)—These are recognized and accepted in all color and marking classes and, with the exception of the crest, to be judged accordingly. Special attention is to be paid to health and normal behavior. The crests are to be distinguished as follows:

1) *Pointed Crest*—Consists of 1 to 60 feathers, either on the forehead or on top of head, growing up from a crown-like base, intertwined and ending in a fine point.

2) *Half-round Crest*—Feathers and crown formation as above but feathers pointing outward and forward so that those on the forehead nearly reach the cere, forming a half-rounded shape similar to a cap visor.

3) *Round or Double Crest*—Feathers as above but formed by two successive double crowns, which can vary in distance (from each other), arrangement and size, so that 2 to 120 feathers are growing in a circular pattern over the top of the head, pointing upward and outward. This growth pattern forms round and double crests of different shapes and sizes. All are officially recognized; they have to be as large as possible, can be inter-connected and symmetrical, or when separated they must have two different shapes, *e.g.*, half-rounded crest and a back mane.

A Harry V. Lacey portrait of a British champion budgie.

Color Varieties of Budgerigars—Their Origin and Development

How do the individual colors of the plumage of budgerigars come about? The basic color of free-living budgerigars is green—a kind of green, which in this particular case arose from a mixture of yellow and blue. The feathers of green budgerigars contain a yellow (fat soluble) color pigment as well as so-called dark colored pigments (melanin). The latter are black and brown pigments in the form of tiny grains. The light reflecting off the feathers undergoes several changes; the red of the spectrum is "swallowed up" by the melanin; the blue light rays return to our eyes; however, they pass through the yellow pigments, which act as a filter, so that we perceive these rays as a pure green coloration.

Those parts of the plumage which contain melanin at the surface layer tend to swallow up the yellow. The melanin grains occur in different sizes, forming a variable arrangement in the plumage. This explains the diversity of the markings from black to brown to dark gray, and on to light gray and a pale gray.

In pure yellow budgerigars (lutinos, yellow black-eyes) the melanin is absent. The same applies for the light feather patches among the pied forms.

Therefore, budgerigars' colors consist of relatively few "building blocks" which, when placed together in a variety of different combinations, produce the many different colors seen in these birds today. Birds of the blue series derive their colors from the fact that the "yellow filter" is absent. If the melanins as well as the yellow pigments are absent, we get white birds; gray birds are produced by a different kind of melanin or through a different arrangement of the melanin grains. The so called "blue yellow-faces", which occur in two different mutations, are actually mixed forms. Mutation I has the yellow restricted to the face mask and the bright markings on the shortest, outer tail feathers (in opaline birds coloration of the face mask is extended to most of the head and, therefore, one refers to these as yellow heads). The feathers in the yellow areas contain the yellow color pigment; all other patches which appear blue are missing the yellow pigment. Birds of Mutation II look identical as juveniles; however, after they have obtained the adult plumage a small amount of yellow pigment begins to accumulate in nearly all feathers. This phenomenon increases with advancing age and from one molt to the next. Therefore, light blue adults of this mutation have a turquoise coloration, dark forms appearing to be a mixture of cobalt and turquoise; mauve, gray and aquamarine birds become olive colored. The dark markings on all of these birds get a hint of yellow. Melanin-diluted whiteblues or whitewings produce, when crossed with Mutant I and II, delicate cream to champagne colored forms. This is even more pronounced for albinos, which do not contain any melanin at all. The famous rainbow colored budgerigars arose from a mixture of yellow-face mutants.

Green budgerigars also have blue feathers, those long, median tail feathers and the cheek patches. The long, median tail feathers are turquoise to ultramarine blue, the cheek patches violet. In these cases the horny substance of the tail feathers contains only very little yellow color pigment, and in the feathers of the patch it is completely absent. Besides, the cheek patches are totally differently structured. The individual feather branches are stronger and contain pigments clear to the outer margin, so that the blue light rays of the spectrum are totally absorbed and only the violet ones are reflected. In another mutant the appearance of a violet base color has come about under similar circumstances. Moreover, besides the reciprocity of the yellow color pigment and the melanins, the feather structure plays an important role for the color appearance of budgerigars.

GENETICS—THE SCIENTIFIC BASIS
FOR BUDGERIGAR BREEDING

As a modern breeder one cannot ignore the results and consequences of genetics. In order to understand this properly one has to be familiar with the fundamentals of this science. All hereditary elements of each organism are situated in the cell nucleus and occur within the so-called chromosomes. Chromosomes are microscopically small, thread-like structures. These structures and all hereditary elements in them are multiplied through self-duplication. Each organism has in each of these cells a fixed number of chromosomes, which are characteristic for a species. Moreover, the cells of higher plants and animals contain two identical sets of chromosomes. Human body cells, for instance, contain 46 chromosomes, that is two sets of 23 chromosomes each. With the exception of the so-called sex chromosomes, these sets are identical; each chromosome in a particular cell has an equal partner, which contains the same hereditary characteristics.

Cells reproduce through division; before each divides the chromosomes have to be duplicated. After a cell divides each daughter cell contains the daughter chromosomes. This mechanism assures that all cells in each organism contain the same number of chromosomes and thus the same hereditary characteristics. Since the chromosomes are available in two sets, each hereditary characteristic normally occurs twice in each cell. Fertilization consists of the union of a sperm cell and an egg cell, where the nuclei of these two also join. So that it cannot happen under these circumstances that four sets of chromosomes appear, before the egg and sperm cells are formed their chromosome number is halved. In a complicated process called meiosis one cell with two sets of chromosomes produces four cells, each containing only one set. Therefore, the fertilized egg cell then suddenly contains two sets of chromosomes again, one from the female and one from the male. Thus, the embryo will get half of its hereditary characteristics from its father, the other half from its mother. In each set of chromosomes there is one sex chromosome, which determines the sex of a particular organism. One distinguishes between an X chromosome and a Y chromosome. Among birds the Y chromosome determines the female sex, the union of two X chromosomes produces a male (this is exactly the opposite in mammals!). The sperm cells of birds contain in their single set of chromosomes always the X chromosome, the egg cells either the X or the Y chromosome. Therefore, the fertilized egg cell contains either two X chromosomes, producing a male, or it contains one X and one Y chromosome, producing a female.

These details, which may appear complicated at first, are of paramount importance to the budgerigar breeder, since many characteristics are inherited of a sex linked basis, *i.e.,* the hereditary characteristics for a particular trait are carried on the X chromosome. Sex-linked are, for instance, the color varieties of the lutinos and albinos, the lacewings, opalines, cinnamons and slates. As an example let us look at the lutinos.

1. A lutino cock (XX) contains the trait for a lutino characteristic in both X chromosomes, thus it is available in duplicate. The lutino hen (XY) also passes on the lutino characteristics but only in its X chromosome. The entire progeny of such a pair, cocks as well as hens, will then at least obtain one X chromosome. In this particular case the characteristic is inherited pure; 1,0 lutino x 0,1 lutino = 100% lutinos with a sex ratio of about 50 to 50.

2. If the same lutino cock is mated with a non-lutino hen, *e.g.*, with a green hen, the lutino characteristic is then only passed on from the cock to the daughters. The only X chromosome of the green female does not carry the lutino characteristic. The male offspring from such a union receive from the father only one X-"lutino" chromosome. The second X chromosome, which they receive from the mother, does not contain the lutino characteristic. Since light colors are mostly recessive, that is they are dominated by darker colors, the female's green predominates in all male offspring. Although the cocks resemble the female, they can, however, pass on the lutino characteristic from the one X chromosome, which they have inherited from their father. The daughters of such a union, however, have received from their father the X chromosome with the lutino characteristic and from their mother the color neutral Y chromosome. Therefore, the lutino characteristic dominates and is thus externally visible. If we identify the "X" chromosome, which contains the lutino characteristic and that which does not contain this characteristic "x", the genetic formula of the cock would be Xx (in order to avoid confusion we have selected purposely this simpler formulation, which does not conform to the one permanently used in science and in biology textbooks).

3. We now cross a pure-breed green cock (xx = lutino characteristic absent from x chromosome) with lutino hen (XY = lutino characteristic only on X chromosome). The result would be a surprise to the beginner; all offspring, cocks as well as hens, are green. How did this happen?

The lutino mother passes her X lutino chromosome onto her sons, whose formula is Xx, as indicated in example 2. Although the lutino characteristic is still present, it is covered up by the green. The young cocks are green/lutino. Their external appearance (phenotype) is green; however, they are partially lutino. This genetic characteristic is always indicated with a right slash (/) and indicates a color characteristic which is recessive behind the slash in lower case letters. Phenotype and genotype do not necessarily have to be the same as far as the external appearance of an animal is concerned.

Now back to the third example. The daughters cannot inherit from their green father (xx) the lutino characteristic because he does not have it. The lutino characteristics of the mother are tied to the single X chromosome, which is only passed onto the sons (the daughters receive the color neutral, Y chromosome). Therefore, the daughters are also green; that is they are pure-bred green. This now leads us to an important rule, which must be applied to all crossings which have an important sex-linked characteristic. Females, with a sex-linked characteristic which is tied to the X chromosome, can never be genetically segregated. Their phenotype corresponds, as far as the color is concerned, to the genotype.

4. There is an internationally accepted abbreviation to indicate the sex of animals: males are indicated by numbers in front of a comma, females behind the comma. If only one animal is involved a zero is used in front or after the comma. 1,0 indicates a cock; 0,1, a hen; 2,0, 2 males; 0,3, 3 females; 1,1 is a pair; 2,3 is 2 cocks and 3 hens, etc. Therefore, 1,0 Green/lutino is a green cock, genetically segregated in lutino. If we cross such a cock with a lutino female one expects, theoretically, four different kinds of youngsters, in approximate equal proportions; lutino cocks which have received one X chromosome from each parent and are, therefore, phenotypically lutinos (genotype XX = lutino); green cocks which are mixed in lutino (Xx), because they have received one X "lutino" chromosome, while their other x chromosome carries the characteristic for green, which covers the lutino characteristic; lutino females, which have received one X chromosome each from their father and finally green females with an x chromosome from their father, which does not carry the lutino characteristic, together with the color neutral female Y chromosome. These are pure green, although both of their parents could have passed on the lutino characteristic to them.

232

5. The last possibility which remains is the crossing of 1,0 Green/lutino x 0,1 Green (Xx x xY). Such a crossing should produce, theoretically, 25% lutino females where the X "lutino chromosome" of the males meets together with the Y chromosome of the females. The remaining females 25% of the offspring are pure green. Therefore, we find the combination xY. Similarly only half of the expected males are genetically segregated in lutino, those which have inherited the X "lutino chromosome" of the father; it combines with the x of the mother to form Xx. The other half of the males have formula xx; that is they are again pure green.

The above lutino example holds true for all sex-linked color varieties. Once again, below is a tabulation of the results of crosses of opaline birds with those of a normal coloration. Instead of opaline we can also use cinnamon, or albino, or slate, etc.

1,0 opaline x 0,1 opaline = 50% opaline hens, 50% opaline cocks

1,0 opaline x 0,1 normal = 50% normal/opaline cocks, 50% opaline hens

1,0 normal x 0,1 opaline = 50% normal/opaline cocks, 50% normal hens

1,0 normal/opaline x 0,1 opaline = 25% opaline cocks
25% normal/opaline cocks
25% opaline hens
25% normal hens

1,0 normal/opaline x 0,1 normal = 25% normal cocks
25% normal/opaline cocks
25% normal hens
25% opaline hens

Of course, this ratio of progeny from one pair would only be approximated in at least 100 offspring. This holds true for the sex ratio as well as for the color varieties which are sex related. Dominant and recessive inheritance is according to the Mendelian laws. For the already established color varieties DUNCKER in Germany and STEINER in Switzerland had worked out the genetics towards the end of the 1920's. Their results form the basis of later parakeet genetic research and for the additional color mutations. Anybody wishing to explore genetics in greater detail should obtain the handbook by BENL. Dominant or recessive inheritance of plumage colors and marking characteristics are also included in the hereditary genes, which are each available in duplicate. If both genes in one particular individual are identical one refers to this as being genetically pure (breeding true) in contrast to being genetically segregated if both corresponding genes of particular chromosomes are different. If both genes are different only one can dominate with the first crossing. The other genetic hereditary factor remains recessive; that is for the time being it disappears from the phenotype, yet it is being preserved in the bird and again reappears in successive generations. All parakeet color varieties can be bred and combined according to these laws. The effects of dominance and recessiveness can be calculated approximately in advance of the progeny from a particular cross. The color of wild parakeets (normal light green) is dominant over all other plumage colors, with one exception (Australian gray). The blue mutant remains recessive to the green wild color. In genetic terms this can be expressed as follows:

Green x blue = 100% Green/blue (phenotype Green)

Green x Green/blue = 50% pure Green, 50% Green/blue (all phenotypically green; pure forms can only be distinguished from segregated ones through controlled crossing within the next generation). Green/blue x Green/blue = 50% Green/blue, 25% pure Green (both forms indistinguishable), 25% pure Blue (recessive colors, when appearing in phenotype are always pure). Green/blue x Blue =

50% Green/blue, and 50% Blue (which indicates that this cross is more suitable for Green-Blue breeding).

In all of these examples it is irrelevant whether the cock or the hen is green or blue respectively. Our examples hold true for all crosses of a dominant with a recessive characteristic. Apart from the original basic colors, there are three different shades which can be recognized more or less distinctly in all color varieties. These too are genetically dependent. Let us remain with the example of the green budgerigar. It has become common practice to call those genes which produce the different shades, "dark factors." The light green wild form does not have a dark factor. The dark green budgerigar has a dark factor. The commonly used name "dark green" is somewhat misleading. Originally, these birds were referred to as laurel-green. If the dark factor appears pure (in both corresponding genes) the bird is olive-green. Here, once again, are a few practical examples:

Light Green x Light Green = 100% Light Green

Light Green x Dark Green = 50% Light Green and 50% Dark Green

Dark Green x Dark Green = 50% Dark Green, 25% Light Green and 25% Olive-Green

Dark Green x Olive-Green = 50% Dark Green, 50% Olive-Green

Olive Green x Olive-Green = 100% Olive-Green

In the blue series the dark factor affects the colors light blue (dark factor absent), dark blue (one dark factor) and mauve (two dark factors). This gives the following results:

Light Blue x Light Blue = 100% Light Blue

Light Blue x Dark Blue = 50% Light Blue and 50% Dark Blue

Dark Blue x Dark Blue = 50% Dark Blue, 25% Light Blue, 25% Mauve

Dark Blue x Mauve = 50%Dark Blue, 50% Mauve

Mauve x Mauve = 100% Mauve

From that we see that the dark green and dark blue are mixed. They possess only one dark factor and, therefore, individuals which do not receive the dark factor are light green or light blue; individuals which inherit the dark factor in duplicate are olive green or mauve. If one crosses one budgerigar without the dark factor with another budgerigar which possesses both dark factors, then the entire progeny will have one dark factor. This produces the following results:

Light Green x Olive-Green = 100% Dark Green

Light Blue x Mauve = 100% Dark Blue

These crosses are strongly recommended for pure color breeding, because the dark greens and dark blues are very popular because of their strong color. In crosses between green and blue the dark factor is passed on according to the same rules, with one exception. This should be illustrated with a few additional examples of the theoretical expectation of the progeny.

Light Green/blue x Light Green/blue =

        50% Light Green/blue

        25% Light Green (pure)

        25% Light Blue (pure)

Light Green/blue x Dark Blue =

        25% Light Green/blue

        25% Dark Green/blue

        25% Light Blue

        25% Dark Blue

Light Green/blue x Mauve = 50% Dark Green/blue, 50% Dark Blue

Olive Green/blue x Mauve = 50% Olive Green, 50% Mauve

These rules apply for all crossings of budgerigars of the green series with birds from the blue series, independent of sex. They influence the base color only, not the genetically dependent changes of the markings. Similarly for crosses within the green series or the blue series, which all appear in these three different shades and which are bred at the ratios indicated. However, they are difficult to recognize by the untrained eye among the gray green and gray birds. With time every breeder will learn to distinguish light-, medium- and dark gray green, and thus will be able to confirm the inheritance of dark factors among the progeny.

A deviating pattern of inheritance can be observed among dark green budgerigars which have a segregated blue characteristic. This has to be given special consideration. One would normally expect from a cross of dark green/blue x light blue, according to our previous examples, always equal in parts 25% dark green, light green, light- and dark blue offspring. However, as a matter of fact, we will only get about 6.5% light green, 6.5% dark blue and 43.5% dark green and 45.5% light blue, or the reverse; that is 43.5% light green and dark blue, and 6.5% each dark green and light blue offspring. This is brought about by crosswise exchange of factors during cell division (which distributes two sets of chromosomes to four sperm cells with each one chromosome set). At a certain stage during this cell division two corresponding chromosome patterns from each set will be approaching each other closely. This then enables certain sections of these particular chromosomes to be exchanged among them, which then includes those hereditary factors located at these particular sites. This process is known as "crossing over." The somewhat deviating hereditary process among budgerigars of the color variety dark green/blue appears to be caused by such a crossing over. It can also happen that within such a crossing over process dominant and recessive genes are being exchanged.

Dark green/blue budgerigars have the hereditary factors for dark = D and for blue = B. The corresponding recessive partners of these factors have to be designated d and b. A budgerigar of the variety dark green/blue from type 1 will have to be given the genetic formula BD/dd (because this bird has two each of the corresponding chromosomes, which carry the traits for the particular color characteristics). If we then cross this particular bird with a light blue one, the progeny will be predominantly dark green and light blue, and only a few animals will be light green and dark blue. However, type 2 dark green/blue carries on each of the particular chromosomes one dominant and one recessive hereditary factor. This genetic formula is Bd/bD. The composition of the progeny of this bird would be inversely related to the above example.

The process of crossing over, which produces the two different genotypes in dark green/blue, is difficult to understand unless one studies basic cell division. However, this is hardly the place to give a summary of this; those who are interested will find descriptive details in any detailed book on biology. Such books, nowadays, will illustrate it in detail and they are inexpensive.

The results of this process are very important for professional budgerigar breeding. The external appearance of both dark green types is indistinguishable from each other. If their origin is not known we can only tell from the first progeny of certain crosses to which type they belong. Type 1 birds are predominant in crosses where the green parent is darker than the blue one. Crosses where the green parent is lighter than the blue one produce predominantly type 2 offspring. Here are a few examples.

Olive Green/blue x Light Blue = Dark Green/blue Type 1
Olive Green/blue x Dark Blue = Dark Green/blue Type 1
Light Green/blue x Dark Blue = Dark Green/blue Type 2
Light Green/blue x Mauve = Dark Green/blue Type 2

Nowadays, type 2 are far more common than those of type 1. The reason for this is apparently the fact that the sometimes rather small and unattractive olive-green birds have gone out of fashion; they have been replaced by the similar yet more attractive longer gray-green birds. The same holds true for mauve birds relative to gray ones. The dark green budgerigar itself, irrespective of whether from type 1 or type 2, is somewhat difficult as a show bird. Its form and size is often not very satisfactory and the color shade highly variable. The base color is often spotty and, therefore, this bird is never used by show breeders to promote color depth in dark blue and violet birds. Such crosses, again, produce more type 2 dark green birds. Apart from dominant and recessive hereditary characteristics, there is another intermediate hereditary process when breeding budgerigars for color where both of these characteristics are approximately "equally strong." This can be observed particularly when breeding the various pied varieties and their combinations. First, let us consider the example of the recessive pied or harlequin. Among these are very light, that is almost yellow or white birds, as well as very dark ones, nearly green or blue birds with a substantial amount of black markings, and only a very few yellow or white, light plumage patches. (It should be noted here that cocks tend to be lighter than hens.) The show- or color breeders want a bird where the light and dark colors are nearly equally distributed. In order to accomplish that he can use the intermediate hereditary process by using one bird which, according to the standard, is too light and cross this with a dark bird. Approximately 50% of the progeny will then have the desired color and marking. Light and dark have then become combined to produce an intermediate form.

This process can also lead to the formation of other types, which deviate substantially from the parent birds. One of these has been produced by AF ENEHJELM. He started out with a pied bird, the so-called harlequin, and combined this with a continental pied. The harlequin characteristics are passed on recessively and the continental pied characteristics dominantly. What is the result of such a cross? From a recessive harlequin and a dominant (more correctly, partially dominant) continental pied one gets, in the first generation, about 50% dominant pied and 50% birds without color patches. The entire progeny is genetically segregated as far as the harlequin characteristic is concerned. If those birds without color patches are crossed among themselves one gets 50% dark birds (segregated, harlequin), 25% pure dark and 25% pure harlequin. In a subsequent mating within the segregated harlequin dominant pied, the result will come as a surprise. We get about 50% dominant pied in different marking and color stages, 25% non-pied budgerigars and 25% pure yellow birds belonging to the green series, or respectively pure white birds when the original birds belong to the blue series. All offspring have and retain deep black eyes without the light ring around the iris. They also have orange yellow beaks, pink legs and feet, and the cocks will get the pink to weak violet cere, which are all characteristic of harlequin birds with an exception of the plumage markings. Strangely enough, the marking characteristics of both pied forms were not combined genetically, but instead all dark colors and markings were dissolved. What was left was a pure light budgerigar. Genotypically this form remains an intermediate pied, a combination of two different pied races, which in this form will not breed true. If we now cross the light birds among themselves we will not only get 75% light and even dark-eyes, but we also get 25% pure harlequin. Among the light birds there are still 75% which have only one genetic factor for "light" so that in the following generation they will produce another 25% harlequin. Only the remaining 25% of the light birds will have already acquired the two genetic factors for this characteristic. These birds will breed true. In order to get this final result one will require then three generations.

When breeding for size, form and markings the progeny will often be intermediate between the parents, although according to OSER (cited by STEINER) size is a dominant

240

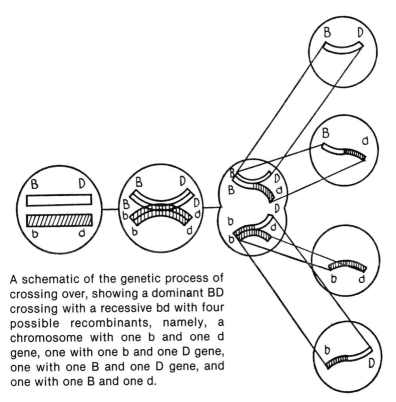

A schematic of the genetic process of crossing over, showing a dominant BD crossing with a recessive bd with four possible recombinants, namely, a chromosome with one b and one d gene, one with one b and one D gene, one with one B and one D gene, and one with one B and one d.

characteristic. Consequently, a breeder with a somewhat small but nevertheless attractive bird in a particular color which he would like to maintain will breed this bird with a very large one. This is done in the hope that at least some of the progeny will then be intermediate to both parent birds. Many breeders who wish to improve the shape of the birds go about it in a similar way, although this does not give the desired results in every case.

Passing on genetically the arrangement and size of throat spots as well as size and extent of the mask also involves this intermediate process of heredity. Budgerigars with normal wave-like markings have a tendency to produce wide masks but at the same time also small, although evenly distributed, throat spots. On the other hand, birds with opaline markings are known in many cases to produce narrow masks but simultaneously large throat spots often arranged in double chains. These unattractive spot accumulations can be eliminated to some degree through crosses of opaline birds with normal birds. At least in some of the progeny the masks appear wide with the desired large, round throat spots arranged symmetrically.

This method may seem simpler than it really is. There are many different genetic factors involved, and the desired combination is still relatively rare. Besides, the normal x opaline crossing tends to produce, unfortunately, quite often an undesired intermediate form; the wave marking on a normal bird must be well defined, black and yellow in the green series, and black and white in the blue series; those of the opaline bird are characterized by black spots with green or blue borders respectively. Among good opaline birds this produces the highly desired opalizing sheen, which has given this color variety its name. Unfortunately, the intermediate form has, quite often, irregular normal markings with opalizing green or blue feather margins. This gives the unharmonious overall impression of a not particularly attractive mixed form, which has rarely ever obtained top scores in a show. Among opaline birds as offspring from normal budgerigars the addition of a black pigment increase from the normal parent bird commonly produces the highly undesired black patches on the back of the head, extending downwards towards the back (the "mantle" referred to in the standard); particularly these plumage areas should be as spotless and clean colored as possible in good opaline birds. Therefore, one has to expect, apart from some good birds, also a fair amount of useless excess birds in continued opaline x normal crosses. This has caused many breeders to produce normal and opaline lines preferably pure, and only occasionally incross their other lines. To those who breed show birds I would like to recommend they follow this same pathway. One gets more experienced with time and eventually learns when a crossing of this kind is more successful.

COLOR VARIETIES OF THE "GREEN SERIES"

The Wild-Colored, Normal, Light Green Budgerigar

This bird is the origin of today's domesticated budgerigars. Many fanciers still consider it to be the most attractive budgerigar. In England it was for a long time the most commonly exhibited bird. It was also the genetic basis for all subsequently developed color varieties. Regrettably, breeders thought that this bird would retain its robust health and fertility, despite intensive inbreeding for the sake of producing a multitude of color varieites. Because of such excesses, the positive breeding characteristics of this bird have become significantly reduced. Later on, this condition was remedied again through incrossing of the (then) popular gray-green birds, increasing the fertility of light green birds. Both colors complement each other rather nicely as far as show standards are concerned.

In the meantime, breeding light green budgerigars has also achieved high standards in Germany. Together with gray birds, the greens are bred very successfully as show birds. Gray-green budgerigars are the only mutants which, when crossed with the wild color, are not necessarily dominant. From a cross light green x gray-green we get, in the first generation, about 50% light green and 50% gray-green birds of nearly equal quality; provided, of course, the parent birds were from pure blood lines. However, in very intense competitions in large shows, the gray-green birds will often do slightly better.

It is advisable to cross light blue birds with this same blood line. It also produces gray birds, and thus we get four different colors of about equal quality. Example:

Light green/blue x light gray green/blue = 32.5% each light green and gray-green, and 13.5% each light blue and gray.

Light green/blue x gray = (about) 25% each in the above four colors.

Pure light green birds are fairly rare these days, because the British race tends to produce sterility in purebred birds. Crossing in blue (or gray, which does not produce any negative effect) promotes color intensity in green and vice versa.

The Dark Green Budgerigar

Most of the more important details about this color have already been mentioned. Mixed colors are somewhat problematic as show birds: they are inclined towards inferior form and size and to show washed out colors. Yet, despite that, there are still breeders with ambitions to produce quality dark green parakeets. This can indeed pay off, because competition in this color class even in large exhibitions is usually small. For the production of good show birds of pure stock, SCHWARZBERG advises against incrossing of blue in order to get a laurel green color without a sheen of blue. Apart from that, one can breed good dark blue birds with the aid of dark green ones. Therefore, versatile show breeders always keep some dark green birds as breeding birds in their aviaries, much less as show birds. Mass breeders cannot do without dark green birds, because they are in demand for producing other bright colors. It is this breeder who has to be familiar with the genetic difference between type 1 and type 2. This is vital for predicting the ratio of segregated light- and dark green, light- and dark blue birds of the progeny.

The Olive-Green Budgerigar

This budgerigar is still fairly rare as a show bird, which is indeed a pity, because its plumage has a very attractive color tone. In high-quality show specimens the somewhat subdued olive green has a silky gloss without any impurities. This color variety is difficult, because it has a tendency toward a dark green spottiness, when crossed with other colors. However, when mated among themselves these birds will become constantly smaller, with an inferior body. Even fanciers, who like tame "talkers", are not too fond of these birds. In show breeding, the gray-green birds have forced the olive-green ones out, because they are fairly similar in their base colors (gray-green birds have a mustard green tone). There are also fanciers of olive-green birds who, despite their segregated genetic characteristic, use these birds for producing improved pure stock colors of other varieties, such as lutinos, dark blue and violet. Therefore, this particular color variety is not expected to die out again that quickly.

Olive-green budgerigars possess a double factor for "dark"; therefore, inbreeding produces genetically pure birds. Olive-green birds are also needed by breeders who work with mauve colors. These two dark colors complement each other rather nicely, eliminating any blotchiness with other tones. Crossing one bird without the "dark" factor (light green and light blue) with an olive-green bird produces 100% dark green or dark blue respectively. This is a definite advantage of selective color breeding.

The Gray-Green Budgerigar

This color variety has been mentioned frequently in this book. It had a meteoric rise, since an Australian breeder discovered this mutation. At first, it was referred to as Australian gray. The first crossing of this mutation with a green budgerigar produced gray-green birds (see also "light green budgerigar"). Shortly thereafter it was discovered that the "dark" factor influences the gray-green and gray, as well as all other colors. Medium gray-green becomes a shade darker; dark gray-green is even darker with a hint towards olive-green. The genetics of passing on the dark factor from one generation to the next is the same in all colors. The gray cheek patches and the black tail feathers are the same in all shades of gray-green. Only segregated blue, and to a larger extent violet birds, sometimes have a touch of blue or violet in these plumage areas.

Gray-green is the budgerigar color most suitable for the desired standard; it is also a large, massive bird with a broad, high head. Therefore, gray-green birds are frequent winners at famous shows. In addition, this color variety also serves to improve many other color standards. Unfortunately, this has not been to this bird's advantage. Anyone believing that via the gray-green coloration an unlimited number of standard birds could be produced was badly mistaken. It is, therefore, quite common to find some very good birds of this color but also others which have, apart from their coloration, little in common with standard budgerigars. The beginner is, therefore, warned against paying too much attention to the color when purchasing gray-green birds, because there are rarely ever any flaws in it.

When breeding gray-green, either pure or by crossing them with grays, the first generation produces 25% gray-greens (or grays) with the double factor passed on dominantly and in full. If gray-green with the double factor is crossed with a different green, the first generation progeny consists 100% of gray-green birds. These, of course, have only a single factor for "gray-green." If these are then again bred with other greens, the offspring are then segregated again into gray-greens, light greens, etc. After all, gray-green is just as dominant over gray as is green over blue.

The Opaline Green Budgerigar

This form of melanin reduction is most visible on head and neck. There, the bold black and yellow markings of normal birds are reduced to weakly gray thin lines against a yellow base color, which should ideally blend into a pure green back without any markings. Markings are restricted to the wing covers, while the otherwise dark feathers have a medium pale gray cross band; the breeders refer to this as the "mirror." The long, dark tail feathers have a light margin along the shaft. This, incidentally, is another manifestation of melanin reduction and it is not considered a flaw, as long as the entire feathers are not lighter than the base color. A fault, not too uncommon in opaline birds, is a base color which is overall too light. In depth and intensity it should be identical to that in normal budgerigars.

The positive and negative effects of crossings between opaline birds and normal ones have already been reported. Generally speaking, there are now more good opaline birds than normal birds among the British show race. The very heavy opaline gray-greens and light greens are also very popular in Germany now. These birds, however, have a tendency towards washed out back markings, together with a rather untidy plumage. They leave much to be desired in vitality and fertility. Therefore, it is imperative that the more delicate and smoother yellow variety not be forgotten when producing opaline lines. Its success depends upon frequent incrossing with yellow birds. If, in addition a particularly pure, bright green back plumage is desired, incrossing with the more spectacular royal opaline is recommended. This variety is currently only bred by fanciers who are especially interested in colors, although these extremely colorful birds would find a ready market among those who are interested in "talkers." The royal opaline surfaced as a mutation in Belgium during the 1930's, but it seems to have been forgotten again now by most mass breeders, although it reappears occasionally.

The royal opaline is distinguished from the common opaline by the presence of a pure yellow head, a nearly pure green back, a wider "wing mirror" and finally by different markings on the wing covers. The wing butt and the largest part of the shoulder feathers are both almost completely without black patches and they strongly opalize. The disadvantages of this bird are: it tends to produce small sizes, narrow heads, small throat spots and tail feathers which are too light. Its plumage is very fine and the bird, therefore, appears less voluminous. It lacks even more pigmentation than the common opaline bird, while the modern show opaline has too much of it in its especially large throat spots.

British show standards do not recognize the royal opaline, while it is commonly accepted on the Continent. Many of the top breeders believe that the existing stock of excessively large, rough plumaged opaline breeds should be further increased, before its colors and markings are improved through large scale incrossing. Such improvement is urgently needed, because some of the more recent imports from England have shown a highly undesirable characteristic: a very unattractive dark blotchiness on the forehead. This surfaced once before during the 1950's, and it took years to remove this dominantly inherited trait from the existing blood lines. Now it appears to have crept in again. This flaw is particularly widespread among hens, especially among those with superior type, size and head form. Under these circumstances one can, of course, only use birds with clean foreheads for further breeding, and use yellow-type-opaline and royal opaline birds for increased incrossing. Some breeders have had already promising results with this approach. Yet, despite its superior size, head form and type, it also seems to be genetically interconnected with forehead blotchiness, which tends to create conflicting situations for exhibitors and breeders alike.

Graywinged Green Budgerigars

This is a fairly old mutation which, during the 1920's, appeared simultaneously in several countries. At first, it was called "apple green" because about 50% of these birds had a light base color, which resembled that of green apples. Wing- and wave markings are gray-yellow; the shades of colors in light, medium and dark are clearly recognizable. They conform to normal colors, yet they are about 50% "diluted." The cheek patches are paler than those in normal birds, with a tinge of gray in them. The primaries and long tail feathers are smoke gray, the latter with a tinge of blue.

Today there are only few devotees of graywings and, therefore, the original form of this bird is becoming increasingly
rare. It is less suitable for shows; most specimens are too
small and fragile. Genetically they are recessive to normal
birds. Graywings x normal, produces 100% normal/gray-
wings. If these are interbred, we get 25% graywings, etc. In
order to determine the other results of such a cross, one can
refer to the examples given for the green-blue inheritance.

Lightwing Budgerigar, Green Series, often called "Green Yellow-wing"

This mutation was developed in the 1930's by Australian
breeders. Because of its conspicuous color contrast, this
rather small, insignificant bird caused considerable excitement. It has remained small in body. There is a club in England completely devoted to the breeding of lightwings. In
Germany, there are also many devotees, although they have
had considerable difficulty in obtaining significant show
achievements. However, since the introduction of the placing system within a show class according to colors, this has
changed. Now the best lightwing within its class will get a
first prize, regardless of the other standard qualities relative
to other races, which are superior in size, head shape, etc.
The relevant standard description outlines the appearance of
the ideal green lightwing.

These birds do not have pure yellow wings and, therefore,
the name "lightwing" is more appropriate. The wings
always have faint gray markings, yet somewhat coarser than
graywings with a checkerboard pattern. The cheek patches
are intensive violet, as in normal birds. The throat
spots—they are not always present in the required number—-
are as smoke-gray as in graywings but somewhat paler. Good
specimens show the same color intensity as normal birds;
their primary flight feathers are pale gray, and the long tail
feathers are bluish gray.

1. The beautiful head of a British champion. 2. Body shot of an American-type champion. 3. Newer varieties under development. 4. The trophies before they are awarded at a typical budgie show.

Today's lightwing breeders are already satisfied if they can produce a bird which is sufficiently strong, of a good type and with a well-shaped, not-too-small head. In order to regularly breed this bird in at least modest quantities, the breeder has to maintain practically two separate stocks of birds: one lightwing race and a race of the best and heaviest normal birds of some of the common light or medium colors. Gray-green birds are also quite suitable for that purpose, because they can immediately improve the type and size. However, the breeder is advised to use only a stock which has a single factor for color (heterozygous), because otherwise too many gray-green yellow-wings will be produced. These, of course, do not have such an effective color contrast as the light yellow-wings, or even the dark green yellow-wing. Lightwings are genetically recessive to normal birds, intermediate to graywings but dominant over yellow with white (and white with blue) wings.

With the aid of large normal birds the lightwing breeder can improve the type and size of his birds, but it requires the dominant genetic color characteristics of two generations. Moreover, this cross partially reduces the desirable wing color contrast in the first progeny. However, should he be able to get type-correct, heavy yellow birds—commonly referred to as normal yellow—then the first generation will have yellow-wings, because normal yellow is recessive to lightwings. Furthermore, this color variety does not have a significantly negative influence over the color contrast of yellow-wings. These birds are becoming increasingly popular again. In fact, there is a club in England dedicated to the objective to restore the quality of the formerly well-known British "Buttercup" Budgerigar.

Summarizing then: yellow birds can be bred jointly with yellow-wings in the same stock, because these two varieties complement each other very effectively. The yellows have to be of good standard quality, although they can vary as far as their markings and color are concerned. Before the pure yellow lutinos became popular, the British had tried to breed from the normal yellows, which usually have faint gray ghost markings on their back with a green sheen on their tail coverts, a pure yellow bird, which they called "Buttercup." These yellows occur in three different shades, depending on whether they have two dark factors, one or none. Briefly: the bright yellows are yellowish green, the dark yellows are greenish yellow, and the (rarely available) olive yellows are greenish golden. The tail coverts in all three varieties are of a darker green, and the wave markings vary from pale gray to deep gray. One generally distinguishes between yellows with a strong and weak greenish tone.

The cheek patches are much paler than those in light-wings. The so far mentioned weaker color forms can also be bred in opaline birds. Then the light yellows and gray-yellows look quite nice in their uniform pastel colors. All other varieties are less typical and they are, therefore, rarely bred. The normal yellows are rarely bred on a commercial scale, since they are not in demand as "talkers." However, there is a strong demand for lightwings so that those specializing in breeding this bird will rarely ever have any difficulty in disposing of the progeny, which are inevitably small in body and lack color contrast.

Lutinos

They are the next step in line toward brightening up the colors of budgerigars. They do not have any color pigments at all, apart from the fat soluble yellow color. Therefore, these birds have red eyes (because of the blood shining through), orange-yellow beaks, pale pink legs and feet; the cere of males is pale pink to weak violet.

The first lutino hens are alleged to have appeared around 1870, but these disappeared again, since at that time there was nothing known about sex-linked genetics. Lutinos reappeared again in the 1930's, at first in Germany (lutino from

This champion of champions in the 1960's (front view of the facing page, side view above) may have been an ideal type then; now in the 1980's standards have changed, but this is still a very lovely budgerigar. Photos by Harry V. Lacey.

lutein = yellow color substance). Many budgerigar fanciers consider this egg-yolk yellow bird the prettiest of all budgerigar varieties. Some of the best lutinos now compete effectively in size and type with some of the best show birds. In fact, in the face of stiff competition many of them have won in major exhibitions. However, breeding lutinos is not as easy as a beginner would like to believe. Although these birds are not required (by standard) to have throat spots and other markings, their very fine plumage gives the appearance that they have a smaller body and a smaller head than they really do. Moreover, they develop slowly, so that it takes a long time for them to reach show size and sexual maturity; moreover, lutinos are not overly productive. The color has to be deep yellow over the entire body and it must be free of any greenish sheen, which has a tendency to "creep" into the tail coverts in fully mature birds. Markings are absent. Cocks sometimes have very faint (too obvious for show purposes) yet clearly distinguishable ghost markings.

There is no other budgerigar color variety where the yellow-buff theory is more apparent than in lutinos. The "yellow" bird is the only one which is truly golden yellow. Since it has very fine plumage it appears to be smaller, just as in canaries. Buff lutinos are heavier and usually of a better type, but they are straw-yellow. Both forms are required for breeding. The intermediate forms, which are predominantly cocks, have the best chances at exhibitions. They show a pure, deep yellow, which may not be egg-yolk yellow, yet the birds are of good shape and size. According to the latest official standards, the straw-yellow birds also have excellent exhibition chances provided they are of a superior type.

In most thoroughbred stocks, lutinos breed true, *i.e.*, lutinos are mated with lutinos. Rarely is any incrossing of new blood required, and if needed, one uses preferably normal yellow budgerigars, as long as these are long and strong and of a pure color. Green birds are also suitable for that purpose.

When mated with lutino cocks, light or dark green hens will produce lutino daughters. Yet a lutino hen, when mated with a green cock will only produce lutinos in the second generation. Many breeders believe that the undesirable greenish sheen in lutinos is the result of incrossings with light green birds. This is not necessarily the case. Although dark green produces a more intensive yellow, an even better yellow comes from olive-green. However, the latter supplies—genetically—insufficient size and shape. Gray-green would be the more suitable partner, and in fact many excellent lutinos are bred this way. The only disadvantage is that these birds have a duller, more mustard-like yellow. Lutinos can cover up any color of the green series with or without dark factors, creating phenotypes which vary only very slightly in shades of yellow. Yet this suppression reappears immediately when a lutino is crossed with a dark colored budgerigar. If, for instance, a lutino cock covers light green, its sons from a cross with a light green hen will all be light green. The lutino daughters once again cover light green. With an olive-green hen they would all be dark green or, respectively would cover up dark green, etc. It can, therefore, happen that dominantly reproducing gray-green, when mated with a lutino, may have in the first generation also gray-green lutinos, *i.e.,* those birds which are mustard-yellow and of a usually good type and shape, although their color may not be satisfactory. Yet, these very birds could be very valuable when they are crossed with a lutino, which suppresses another color. About 50% of such progeny does not cover the gray-green and will be intensely golden yellow; these birds will have also inherited the excellent type and size of the gray-green birds.

Opaline budgerigars, irrespective of their variety, should not be crossed with lutinos. Opaline-covering lutinos often display a green sheen in their back plumage; cinnamon and graywings can possibly reduce the intensity of the base color.

Opaline Cobalt. Good size, color and markings. Excellent spots. Lacks frontal rise. Bad stance due to fright.

Opaline Cinnamon Skyblue. Good color and markings, good head and deportment. Color somewhat patchy, multiple spots.

Normal Grey. (Light phase). Good color and markings. Faulty stance, drooping tail, flat head, irregular spots.

Normal Mauve. Patchy color, no spots. Head small, lacks frontal rise. Tail faulty. Not in show condition.

Yellow Face Opaline Mauve.
Good size and color. Bad
stance, head too small,
multiple spots.

Opaline Skyblue. Good
size, color and markings.
Nipped in neck. Irregular
spots. Hangs over perch.

Normal Light Green. Good
type throughout. Good
head. Color slightly
patchy. Spots irregular.
Mask could be deeper.

Normal Violet. Fine color,
good type, markings and
stance. Lacks in top skull,
depth of mask and size of
spots.

Breeders in Holland have been very successful with in-crosses with the dominant Australian pied, as far as the primary feathers are concerned. Common lutinos usually have predominantly white or nearly white primary flight and tail feathers. Some of the lutinos, which cover Australian pied, also have a specially intensive yellow throughout their plumage as well as in their primary flight feathers and in their tail feathers. This creates the impression of a pure-colored, light budgerigar. The pied condition cannot be recognized in these birds.

Lutinos should not breed until they are a year old. Prior to that they are neither fully grown nor ready to breed. There-fore, older birds will be rated higher at shows in the combin-ed classes than birds which are less than a year old. In other words, young and old birds should not be mixed.

Regrettably, lutinos are inclined to incur prolonged eye in-fections, which are often difficult to cure despite the applica-tion of antibiotic ointments. The exact cause is not yet known.

Cinnamon Colored Budgerigars

From the light birds of the green series, let us now sidestep to those with brown pigmentation, all of which have more or less the same base color. Cinnamon colored budgerigars are very popular as show birds; they follow closely behind the normal budgerigar and the opalines. They can be bred in all color varieties, yet the delicate cinnamon-brown markings and the throat spots remain virtually unchanged. Independent of the base color, cocks have a tendency towards darker markings, which are not in accordance with the standard. Therefore, one should mate a very dark quality cock with a hen which has very pale markings, in order to obtain the de-sired cinnamon-brown tone. The primary feathers are al-ways gray-brown, and the long tail feathers are dark to violet-blue, with a brownish shaft. The base colors must be as in-tense as those in normal birds, although this breeding objective is rarely achieved. More commonly the base color is paler, which is quite natural since the cinnamon factor possesses a color-diluting influence. Therefore, among cinnamon colored birds it is even more important than in normal birds to use frequent incrosses with birds from the blue series in order to improve the base colors (the reverse is true for cinnamon-blue birds). Cinnamon colored birds have a tendency towards small throat spots.

Cinnamon light greens are indeed a pleasure to look at, if their delicate brown markings are set against a true grass-green color. Cinnamon dark green birds can even be more attractive, because of such contrast, yet their base color is often spotty yellow or has different shades of green. However, as in all budgerigars with a dark factor, these birds are more difficult to breed true and to maintain type and size. Cinnamon-olive-green budgerigars have a beautifully golden color tone throughout their whole plumage. However, since they are, as show birds, too small, they are rarely seen, because most breeders are not that intensively involved with the reproduction of dark colors. Breeding the sex-linked genetic characteristic of cinnamon is not particularly difficult, provided the breeder starts out with a cock. A cinnamon dark green cock, when mated with an olive-green hen produces, for instance, in the first generation several cinnamon-olive-green hens. Such birds are still relatively rare. The main reason for this may be the popularity of cinnamon-gray-green birds. These birds have a similarly warm color tone throughout their plumage, but they appear somewhat duller. However, as far as their type, size and head shape are concerned they are, in most countries, one of the leading show birds.

The cheek patches of cinnamon-gray-greens are light gray, and the long tail feathers are nearly pure medium brown. The base color is a light mustard-green, with a hint of brown; this is a good match for the light brown-cinnamon markings and primary flight feathers.

Opaline Olive Green. Good size, type and color, though the latter somewhat patchy. Good hen's head, nipped in neck.

Opaline Grey Green. Good color, size and markings. Fairly good spots. Lacks frontal rise. In momentarily bad stance.

Yellow Face Skyblue (Type II). Very good even color and markings. Too small throughout. Lacks frontal rise. Spots too small.

Normal Dark Green Cock. Excellent in type and stance. Good head. Color slightly patchy. Mask and spots slightly uneven.

A young blue budgie in a proud pose. Photo by Aaron Norman.

Opaline Cinnamon-Gray-Green Budgerigars

An even larger success as show birds are the opaline cinnamon-gray-green birds. Most show champions in England, Holland and in Germany (East and West) have in recent years come from this color variety. Therefore, this bird must be discussed in some detail.

The combination of two sex-linked mutations is not as complicated and difficult as it may seem. Here are a few examples. 1,0 cinnamon-gray-green x 0,1 opaline light green = normal gray-green and normal light green cocks, which are segregated in the cinnamon and in opaline characteristic, and cinnamon-gray-green and cinnamon light green females.

1,0 normal cinnamon light green/opaline x 0,1 cinnamon-gray-green = 50% cinnamon in gray-green and light green cocks and hens. Of these about 13.5% are cinnamon opaline gray-green and cinnamon light green hens, 50% light green and gray-green, of these all cocks are segregated in cinnamon, some also in opaline (externally not recognizable).

1,0 normal light green/cinnamon and opaline x 0,1 cinnamon opaline gray-green = 100% cinnamon: cocks and hens in normal cinnamon light green and normal cinnamon-gray-green. Opaline cinnamon light green and opaline cinnamon-gray-green in about equal proportions.

1,0 Opaline cinnamon-gray-green x 0,1 opaline cinnamon light green = 100% opaline cinnamon of both sexes in cinnamon light green and cinnamon-gray-green. There are so many cinnamon opaline birds around that breeders can do without the crossing as indicated in example 1. However, this example has shown how the cinnamon opaline birds were obtained, starting out with normal cinnamon and green birds. At the same time gray-green was added, because cinnamon opaline birds are among the most popular color races. For details please refer to the respective color standard. The three shades: light, medium and dark are among cinnamon opaline gray-greens even less distinct than they are in normal and opaline gray-green birds with black markings. They are present and they will be passed on relative to the strength of the dark factor.

Dark factor absent: light

Single dark factor present: medium

Double dark factor present: dark

After the cinnamon opaline gray-green, the cinnamon opaline light green is the most popular bird today. Many good show birds of this kind can now be seen commonly in large shows.

Generally speaking, cinnamon budgerigars have very dense plumage. Therefore, they have been used for years to improve the plumage of other varieties. However, the careless mating for generations of buff birds among each other has led to long, shaggy feathers. Unfortunately, many such birds can be seen at shows, and yet many judges still have a tendency to give high marks, although the true characteristic of a cinnamon colored budgerigar—smooth, silky plumage, brown pastel color—appears to have been lost in such birds.

If particular attention is being paid so that "yellow" birds are frequently crossed with "buff" birds, cinnamon parakeets remain very productive and can be mated without adverse effect among each other, for the purpose of improving size, shape and color.

Fallow Budgerigars

Just as with lutinos and albinos, these birds too have red eyes and coffee-colored markings. The base color is about two-thirds suppressed. Thus, green fallows, irrespective of color shade, appear predominantly yellow. Only the tail coverts still show the original base color. It is this particular area where we can see that fallow budgerigars occur in all base colors and shades. Fallow parakeets used to be very popular in Germany, especially the yellow ones, which were called golden fallows. From among these the opaline yellow fallows seem to be the more preferred birds. In these the

Left: Yellow Wing Light Green. *Right:* Graywing Olive Green.

Left: Whitewing Skyblue. *Left:* Normal Graywing Skyblue.

Opaline olive green cock, British show quality. Photo by Harry V. Lacey.

brown markings are restricted to wings and throat spots, while the remaining plumage is nearly pure yellow. The large feather of all fallows is of a shade darker (brown) than is seen in cinnamon birds; it forms an attractive contrast to the light base color.

Fallows reproduce pure recessively (covering characteristics). Theoretically, they can be bred in all shades of green and blue, but only experts can detect the subtle differences.

There are not too many breeders specializing in fallows. They are difficult to breed as show birds as far as type and size are concerned. Fallows have a tendency to regress back to the small original type. Besides, fanciers prefer strong and pure light colors in their cage birds. Parallel to the development of the continental fallow of German origin, another genetically recessive fallow race was established in the British Isles. The continental fallow has—just as with lutinos and albinos—a pearl-colored iris ring, but the British birds have pure plum-colored eyes. These birds have never been popular, and they are considered to be nearly extinct now. Apparently different genetic factors were responsible for the origin of continental and British fallows: crosses between both races produced pure green progeny, which separated again into both forms. There are a few breeders in Holland and Germany who cultivate the continental fallow as a show bird. These birds can only be bred from first-class show birds in normal and opaline. As is with all difficult, recessive color races, they do not produce consistently high quality progeny. This means frequent backcrossing of the best segregated bird with the best fallow. This is a long and drawn out process because practically two different blood lines are required. Still, many birds of inferior quality are being produced, and these can only be disposed of through the pet trade. Just as with lutinos and albinos, fallow cocks have a pale pink cere and they can only be sexed fairly late as subadult birds. The horny parts (beak yellow, legs pink) also resemble those of albinos and lutinos.

Lacewings

This is the latest mutation, with weak brownish wave markings against a yellow background, with red eyes and usually silky white cheek patches. The name refers to a lace-like pattern on top of the wings, that is, those faint brown—located far apart—wave markings. Lacewings originated from lutinos and cinnamon, during the 1950's in England. They simply represent the cinnamon form of lutinos. It has been shown that many lacewings came from crosses of cinnamon x lutinos, with dominant cinnamon characteristics.

So far, lacewings have not become too popular in Germany, maybe because they remind people too much of the notorious lutinos with those ghost markings. In contrast to their brownish markings, lacewings have pure white or beige-colored feathers.

Opaline lacewings have uneven and spread out opaline markings.

Recessive Pied Budgerigars or "Harlequins"

This form has already been discussed in some detail in the chapter on genetics. It appeared first in Denmark and was produced by the well-known specialist AF ENEHJELM. Because of their truly colorful harlequin plumage, these birds were in strong demand after the Second World War in Europe and later on in the United States. They were very productive and full of vitality, and they have remained so to this day, although they have resisted standard demands for form and size improvement for a long time. Apart from the pied coloration, the common harlequin strongly resembles the Australian wild budgerigar. Color intensity should not become a concern, as long as other varieties with weak markings are being used for incrossing. It is not even necessary to cross birds from the green series with those from the blue series: one will always get very intense colors, be this light green, dark green, olive-green, etc.

Normal Yellow. Very good type and size. Color appears almost olive. Markings too dark for Buttercup.

Greywing Olive Green. Very good color and markings. Lacking badly in frontal rise. Shows long flight characteristics.

Yellow Face Greywing Sky-blue (Type I). Good color and stance. Markings excellent. Excellent condition. Tail drooped.

Greywing Cobalt. Satisfactory color and markings but extremely long-flighted, hence bad stance. Head too flat and small. Spots too small.

270

Yellow wing light green British show quality budgerigar. Photo by Harry V. Lacey.

Breeding pieds with pieds or with non-pieds does not influence pure colors. In fact, in mass production for the pet trade ("talkers") pure pied crosses are often preferred, because all recessive traits are passed on true. Thus, harlequin x harlequin produces 100% harlequin progeny.

More difficult is the constant reinforcement of the spot-like markings on the back of these birds, together with an even, dark abdominal coloration. Harlequins never look alike, which is a particular stimulus for many breeders. Generally speaking, the cocks have nice spot-like markings on their backs, but the abdominal plumage is interspersed with light feathers, especially at the hind flanks. There is no clear delineation between the light breast and the dark abdomen.

Most hens have, on their backs, unattractive continuous patches consisting of dark markings. These also extend onto the wings. The abdominal color is pure dark, and the rump has usually better delineation between light and dark than is found in cocks.

Much depends on the breeder's ability to select a partner which produces well-marked progeny. Many cocks have only a few tiny dark spots on their back, as well as a dark patch—the size of a five-cent piece—on their abdomen. They are really too light to produce the desired 1:1 color. They are just the right partner for hens which are too dark, however, if well-marked progeny is desired. If from these offspring a few, sufficiently lightly colored hens are mated with cocks which are too dark, the offspring will consist mostly of well-marked, attractive birds. Such birds are very much in demand today.

The genetic principles involved in the inheritance of the dark factor are the same for all pied base colors as well as for normal birds. A pair of light green harlequins produces only light green birds; dark greens give rise to various shades of green; and olive-green birds always produce more of the same. Gray-green pieds can be bred according to the same method as common gray-greens. In this case, the gray-green coloration is also dominant, and the dark green can give a very attractive contrast to pure yellow. The yellow plumage areas are about the same in all shades of green pieds. The yellow color intensity varies slightly between buff and yellow birds (a more intense yellow).

Opaline harlequins can be bred the same way as common opalines. These birds are particularly attractive, because their spots in the back feathers and wings have a bright green margin. Cinnamon harlequins with brown spots are also very attractive, because the color intensity of the green base color remains undiminished. Here, special attention has to be paid, more so than for common cinnamons, that these birds do not become too pale; otherwise there is insufficient contrast with the yellow color.

Reproduction of cinnamon harlequins is according to the same genetic rules as for common cinnamons; however, cinnamon x cinnamon should not be mated. Breeders also have to be cautioned against crossing-in graywings, light wings and all other varieties with thinned out markings. This would produce a typical pied, without color contrast. Therefore, international show standards recognize harlequins only up to the marking reduction in cinnamon. All other varieties have to be exhibited in the AOC class (any other color-class), a collective group for unusual colors.

Breeding show harlequins in British race standard type is very difficult. Only a few dedicated breeders are doing this. This kind of problem is encountered with all recessive forms and, therefore, the same applies to what has already been said about light wings and fallows (see relevant sections). It requires two separate blood lines: high quality attractively marked harlequins and a first-class stock of show birds in normal coloration. The show bird stock should, ideally, come from gray- and light greens, opalines with good heads, possibly also cinnamons of equal quality. In such a mating, the sex is essentially irrelevant; yet experience has shown that hens pass on size and type better than cocks. Conse-

Opaline cobalt cock budgerigar, show quality British bird. Photo by Harry V. Lacey.

Normal Cinnamon Grey-green. Excellent color and markings, excellent type. Dropped tail due to fright Spots irregular.

Yellow Wing Dark Green. Excellent color and good contrast in wings and body color. Lacks type, stance and head qualities.

Normal Cinnamon Violet. Good markings and fair color due to patchiness. Head too small. Stance not correct.

Whitewing Cobalt. Excellent color. White wings satisfactory. Good type though head could be larger.

quently, it is better to use a first-class hen of the British race (ideally, the coarse buff type) together with a harlequin cock. The progeny will not have the pied condition. Most of the young will be intermediate to their parents in type and size; *i.e.,* they will not be as good as their mother but will be better than their father. A minority will be inclined towards the small wild type, and another minority towards the large show type. All offspring are segregated in harlequin, however, and the experienced breeder will, of course, only use birds from this minority for the production of good show birds. These are then mated among themselves. So that no siblings are used for this next step, it is useful to start out initially with as many unrelated pairs of pied x non-pied. The second mating will produce 25% harlequin, and—with a bit of luck—some birds will have a better standard quality than the original harlequins used for establishing this stock. There is little doubt that most harlequins which become class and show winners have been bred this way. The crux of the problem lies in maintaining this quality by further breeding with it. If these birds are mated among themselves one gets a progeny which is inferior in type, size and head shape to the parents. Therefore, continued incrossing from non-pied bloodlines is required in order to maintain the high quality of this stock. Determined breeding efforts can lead to a point where one—apart from the above matings—also mates segregated birds and harlequin birds (because of the favorable size inheritance, the segregated partner should, again, be a hen). In fact, there are already some breeders who have mated harlequin x harlequin with good success. This, of course, requires very high quality in the original pair. The non-pied partner does not have a negative influence on the arrangement of the pied markings. Budgerigars which are segregated in harlequin can often be recognized by a small light spot on their neck. If they are not superior in all other characteristics, they should not be exhibited. In the class for normal birds, the above-mentioned spot will be penalized.

Because of the latest revision of standards and the re-arrangement of show classes the difficult harlequin production has become more interesting and rewarding for many breeders. Consequently, this attractive bird is now seen more commonly in exhibitions. A clear delineation between chest and abdominal coloration is not absolutely necessary, and it is now irrelevant how many spots a harlequin bird has. Some dark markings among the primary feathers are also permissible. In fact, small dark patches at the end of the primary flight feathers and on the tail feathers are quite suitable for a harlequin bird, together with its "own" silver-white interspersed cheek patches, which were always one of the most attractive features of this bird.

Dominant (Continental) Pied, Neck-Spot Pied

All these forms belong to the same color race. The different names tend to confuse the beginner, and for practical reasons these birds are no longer shown in separated classes.

They are the oldest pied form of budgerigars, and they originated in Holland. As with all other budgerigars, these too can be bred in all colors. Their individual markings are highly variable, yet they are all characterized by the presence of a light, thumbnail-sized neck spot. "Light wings" refers to a non-pure breeding sub-group within this race, which was once very widespread.

Dutch pieds were very popular, as long as they did not have to compete with the two other pied forms. Today they are rare; strangely enough in their native Holland they have become extinct. Genetically, they reproduce dominantly, independent of their light and dark colors and markings. The overall coloration and markings are highly variable, to the surprise of many—even experienced—breeders. Thus, a dark bird with a tiny neck spot, when mated with a non-pied partner, can have progeny which are much lighter. On the other hand, one can also get only very few light chicks from a very

Fallow Yellow Green.
Good color and markings.
Lacks type and size bad-
ly. Head and spots much
too small.

Fallow White Cobalt.
Good color and markings
but bad type. Too small,
bad head with protruding
beak, lacking in spots.

Dark-eyed Clear White.
Combination of dominant
and recessive Pied factors.
Good color but small in
body. Tail droops so
stance incorrect.

Lutino. Good size and excellent color. Slightly
heavy, hence faulty stance.
Good large head but lacks
frontal in this shot.

Yes, this is a budgerigar. It was first displayed in England in 1960 where it was nicknamed a "duster." The color of the bird is a normal gray. It has not become a popular breed. Photo by Harry V. Lacey.

light bird. Among these may well be some which have only a neck spot, of variable sizes.

Nevertheless, the majority of these pied budgerigars display a certain system in their pied markings. If the markings go beyond the neck spot, the light throat color extends into a similarly white chest. Sometimes the light neck spots extend to the upper back region and between the shoulders.

Furthermore, there may be some light flank- and tail covert feathers, and some individuals have light primary flight- and tail feathers. This then is the transitional form toward light wings. Here the breeding objective is: at least seven light primary flight feathers, without any dark ones interspersed; the two long tail feathers must be pure light. These birds are also permitted to have a mask extending down to a light bib, as well as some light patches among the small feathers. Such birds are difficult to produce. The most promising method is to mate a good light wing with a non-pied parakeet. However, if two light wings are mated, the offspring are, invariably, too light, with light patches and spots, and with the overall colors not clearly delineated. In fact, this is the greatest disadvantage when breeding this pied form. In addition, there is also the frequently washed out base color. Irrespective of which color shade these birds are being bred—be it light, dark, olive or gray-green—the colors are often so diluted and interspersed with yellow feathers that only an experienced breeder can recognize the birds. Quite often wave markings are so coarse and so extensively penetrated by colored feathers that one often does not know whether this is an opalizing normal bird or whether it is a poor quality opaline parakeet. It is, therefore, more advantageous to specially breed neck spot pieds and light wings in opaline or, even better, in royal opaline.

Prior to the introduction of the British show race into Germany, some breeders had royal opaline light wings which were absolutely spectacular. Some breeders are still clinging to this kind of bird, although their particular form is not in accordance with modern standards. Royal opalines tend to have a finer plumage, narrow heads, a body which is too slim, and throat spots which are too small.

Less difficult are neck spot pieds with normal wave coloration and with common opaline markings. They are easier to breed as show birds than, for instance, recessive harlequins. Shape and size of the neck spot can be rapidly improved by breeding non-pied show birds, especially gray-greens in normal and opaline.

Cinnamon colored neck spot pieds and their light winged form also look very attractive, if the original breeding material was of good quality. Breeders have to be cautioned against incrossings of strongly diluted varieties, such as graywings. Some breeders have tried to achieve brightening up the entire wing, by using a combination of light wings and neck spot pieds. It did work, but the color intensity deteriorated. More promising appears to be the combination of yellows (with green) x light wings; in this case the breeding objective would be the so-called "buttercup" yellow normal bird.

Australian Pied

These birds were established in the aviaries of Australian breeders. Within a few years they have moved to the top of all other pied races. They arrived in England as colorful but small birds. It was then observed that these birds could easily be improved through selective breeding. Here it should be noted that the Australians have traditionally bred for "colors." Most Australian breeders, who attended the world congress of budgerigar fanciers in 1959, considered the ideal British show bird as plump and colorless. Instead, their budgerigars have indeed far brighter colors, but they are also smaller. While the best of these would be able to compete in length with European birds they would be unsatisfactory as far as width, body volume and head are concerned.

Halfsider Recessive Pied Cobalt. Exhibits 5 clearly defined colors. A mutation rarely occurring in this combination.

Dutch Clearflight Normal Light Green. Fairly good in type but lacks in skull and spots. Yellow reaches too far down.

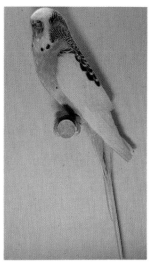

Halfsider Opaline Dark Green-Cobalt. Another unusual, not inheritable, color combination. A well shaped, good sized bird.

Australian Banded Pied Normal Green. Good in color, type and band. Pure, light wings. Lacks size in body, spots, and head.

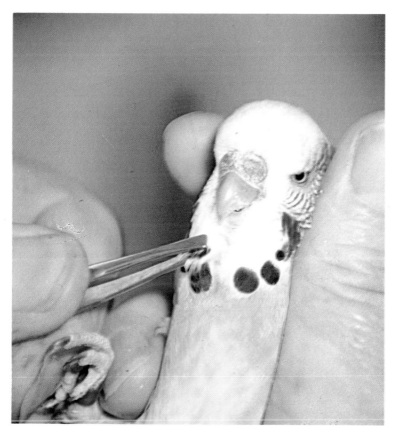

An exhibition hen budgerigar having her mask trimmed. Surplus spots are removed with tweezers leaving only the six best, biggest and most round spots for the show judge to admire. This is acceptable "altering" according to most show rules. Photo by Ray Hanson.

In England, the first Australian pieds were crossed with the best available gray-greens and grays, which produced surprisingly good results; that is, they rapidly approached the European show bird of the British race.

Crosses of Australian pieds with common pieds were very disappointing; the progeny was smaller and less attractive. While the colors remained, several other characteristics combined into a not particularly impressive mixture. Because of these early crossing attempts one still can get unpleasant surprises from allegedly pure Australian pieds. This can include progeny with one white cheek patch and one violet one, or violet cheek patches which are interspersed with white feathers. Even stranger are some offspring from a mating with a harlequin. These may have one black eye, and as the genetic product from the dominant pied, one eye with a light iris ring. Others are completely irregularly marked.

Pure Australian pieds have certain marking characteristics which are peculiar to them. Like the Dutch pieds, they too have a neck spot of variable size but never a light mask extending into the upper breast. Even in the lightest specimens there is always a more or less distinct zone between mask and the rest of the chest and abdominal plumage. The latter has various patches of light feathers. Most birds have clean, light primary feathers (wings and tail), although some dark ones may also be present.

The most distinguishing characteristic of Australian pieds is the double-sized light colored wing butt. The bright plumage area varies in size, from a narrow bright band downwards from the wing butt, toward the point of the outer primary flight feathers to completely light colored wings. Unfortunately, this color pattern is not always symmetrical, and there are indeed birds which have one light colored and one dark wing. At about the middle of the body there is always an area (variable in shape and size) which has light colored plumage. Originally, breeders considered a well-delineated 1.5 to 2.0 cm wide band as the ideal. This gave rise to the names "Band Pieds" or "Banded Pieds" for this color varie-ty. During the early years, the standard even prescribed ten to fifteen points maximum for the band alone. At that time all breeders worked hard to fix this characteristic genetically in their birds. Yet, despite tremendous efforts this has, so far, not yet been accomplished. More successful breeders of Australian pieds cross this bird with a non-pied bird. The progeny is usually satisfactory as far as type, size, color and markings are concerned; however, they have a tendency to be smaller and less attractive. In these birds the light plumage areas are becoming dominant (*e.g.,* the yellow in-creases in green budgerigars). Nowadays, the importance of the band (in terms of point value relative to other character-istics) is not that strongly emphasized any more. An Austral-ian pied must be of good type and have a robust body with a strong head. The chain of throat spots should be as evenly arranged as in non-pied birds.

Type and size should be given preferential consideration over beauty and symmetry when mating pieds. If we then se-lect non-pied birds of standard quality, which are matched in their base color, we can expect—with some luck—a certain percentage of pieds with attractive colors and markings and which are of a good type and size. All that has been said about the green series also applies to the green base colors of Australian pieds. The genetic principles affecting the greens are the same. There is little variation among yellow Austral-ian pieds. Light- and gray-greens are the most popular forms. Many beautiful opaline and cinnamon birds are also bred as Australian pieds. Most fanciers who keep and breed Australian pieds prefer birds with normal black and yellow markings, because such color contrast is very conspicuous. Therefore, Australian pieds are rarely mated with cinna-mons, which tend to dilute the markings. Australian pieds and normal or opaline dark birds, of equal quality, can be bred within the same stock.

Crested Normal Cobalt.
(With neck mane). Rarely
seen visible expression of
2 inheritable factors for
Crested. A new variety.

Half Circular Crested
Normal Cobalt. Good
color and markings. Crest
too small. Lacks in spots.

Tufted Normal Dark Green.
Good size, color and type.
Good crest but skull lacks
width. Spots too small
and irregular.

Tufted Normal Skyblue.
Fair in shape, size and
crest. Color very patchy,
lacks spots. Markings not
clearly defined.

Very beautiful British budgie portrait by Harry V. Lacey.

COLOR VARIETIES OF THE BLUE SERIES

In blue budgerigars the yellow plumage color is absent. Therefore, all areas which are normally yellow are white in blue budgerigars. In normal birds the markings are black and white, instead of black and yellow, and the reduction of white finds its extreme in snow white albinos. For that reason all pieds have white instead of yellow in their light plumage areas. The base colors now change from light green to light blue, from dark green to dark blue, from olive-green to mauve, and from gray-green to gray. Opaline birds have, according to their base color, black wing coverts with blue margins, instead of green margins. Cinnamon colored birds do not change significantly, although the markings appear slightly different against a blue background. Light wings have wings which are more or less whitish gray (instead of yellow wings). They are more correctly referred to as white wings. Fallows and lacewings have brown markings against a white background. Fallows show various shades of blue, particularly on the tail coverts. Just as there are yellow birds with a green rump, there are also white birds with a blue rump. Despite the reduced level of blue, a close examination will always reveal whether these birds are light blue, dark blue or mauve.

The respective standard color descriptions give a good account of the requirements for blue. Here, I would like to concentrate now on the best breeding methods for the various blue color races. Only those forms which have no equivalents in the green series will be discussed in some detail.

All blues are recessive toward greens; they can never be segregated in green. The dark factors behave independently in green- and blue series, with one exception: in dark greens, which are segregated in blue.

If breeding any of the blues is to be successful, the breeder cannot do without greens. Most breeders have blue breeding pairs, which consist of one blue partner and one green, which is a segregated blue. In such mating, sex and other characteristics (normal, cinnamon or opaline) are irrelevant. What has already been said about color reductions and the disadvantages and/or advantages of the various other color forms also applies to the blue series.

Good specimens of dark blues and mauves have always been bred via greens, gray-greens or grays. Show breeders will never mate dark blue x dark blue or light blue x mauve, although quantitatively this produces the largest number of dark blue offspring. Mauve birds are rare as show birds as are olive birds, because their colors have little appeal to most people. The rather similar grays have more to offer and are easier bred in good quality. Thus, one usually finds mauve budgerigars, particularly in the aviaries of "color breeders" who are familiar with genetics, and produce birds as "talkers" for the pet market. Mauve birds are used to produce those colors which are in large demand (dark greens, dark blues, violet). Incidentally, this also applies for the breeding of opalines and pieds in these same colors. Grays are found exclusively, again, with show breeders; these birds are in little demand as "talkers."

Whites with a blue rump or, even better yet, with a gray rump are mainly used for improving the type of blue white wings, just as the yellows in the green series. White-grays in excellent form and size are being exhibited now with increasing frequency.

The albinos have been dropped, somewhat unjustly, by most breeders. It was noted above that in lutinos—as representatives of the green series—it was already more difficult to maintain body volume than in greens, because of the lighter build and finer plumage of lutinos. This is even more true for albinos, as representatives of the blue series. Blues are generally weaker than greens, particularly as far as form and size of head is concerned.

The juvenile plumage is chalk white. As soon as they are fully colored, the tail coverts and flanks, and sometimes the entire underside are delicate blue. This may look pretty, but

Recessive Pied Mauve. Good size, type, color and markings for this difficult-to-breed variety.

Dominant (Dutch) Pied Normal Olive Green. Shows similarity to recessive Pieds in this specimen.

Recessive Pied Yellow Face Blue (Type I). Nice color and markings. Blue could be more extensive. Head small, lacks back skull.

Recessive Pied Skyblue. Nice color and markings, but too small in body and head for exhibition bird.

A very beautiful portrait of an opaline cobalt hen by Harry V. Lacey.

the albino breeder is trying to get a pure white bird. External factors also make it difficult to maintain the white color, particularly in industrial areas. In addition, a hint of blue often destroys the overall positive impression. This problem can only be solved through incrossing with good gray birds. Albinos which are recessive gray do not have the blue sheen. They are white and will remain so. Besides, with some patience, the good type of grays can also be transferred to albinos. The better the original gray bird is, the quicker the entire process is. Since the albino characteristic is sex-linked the objective can be achieved quicker when the breeder starts out with albino cocks and gray hens. If this is done, the first generation will already produce size-improved albino daughters; those birds covering gray will have the desired chalk white color. From gray females with a double factor for gray we get albino daughters which are pure white without the slightest hint of blue, yet most available grays have only one gray factor. The reason for this is that most breeders do not like to breed only grays or gray-green budgerigars but would rather include blue and green ones.

Most cocks of the above-mentioned crosses are segregated in albino. This again produces from grays, with only one factor, blues which are useless for the production of albinos. However, the picture changes in the following generation, when gray albino hens come together with segregated albino gray cocks. Only these should be used for further breeding, but it is required that the previous crosses were all made among blood-unrelated birds, so that no sibling crosses were involved. Breeders should also be cautioned against using even closely blood-related birds; all albinotic animals have a weakened condition. Therefore, albino breeding must be made with a large stock of blood-unrelated birds.

1,0 gray/albino x 0,1 albino (covering gray) = 50% albinos of both sexes and 50% dark birds, *i.e.*, grays and blues in about equal numbers, provided the original gray bird had only one factor. 25% of the grays and albinos now have the double factor for gray, so that the third generation from these birds consists solely of grays and pure white albinos of both sexes. Then we can also risk mating the best albinos among each other, with an expectation to get 100% albino progeny. This will include then relatively many good show birds.

Just as with lutino cocks, many albino cocks have faintly gray "ghost markings" when they get their adult colors. These markings are even more conspicuous against the white background, than against the yellow of the lutinos. Only strict selectivity can eliminate this.

Ultimately, the albino breeder ends up with a stock of albinos and grays, because he will not be able to do without frequent incrossings with grays. This whole process is too boring for many parakeet breeders, and so albinos are bred relatively seldom. Those few birds which are actually exhibited must then compete with highly bred lutinos, against which they have usually very little chance.

Unfortunately, few breeders have ever thought of vitalizing the overall genetic picture of albino stocks, by using opaline grays, cinnamons and cinnamon opaline grays. All these colors have a beneficial influence upon the white albinos. They are the top characteristic of modern budgerigar show breeding, especially cinnamon and gray, which combine nicely to an eye-pleasing pastel color. These birds can be bred the same way, as described for the green series. There are many more possibilities in this area than most breeders imagine.

The albino breeder has to be cautioned against one thing though: the incrossing of greens, gray-green and blues in an attempt to get all common color varieties in the same stock. The offspring may indeed include a few albinos and lutinos of good type, but the greenish sheen in lutinos and bluish sheen in albinos will get stronger.

For breeding birds of the British show race incrosses from the green series are required for all other colors—not only for

Various genetic factors are apparent in the budgies shown here.

Australian Dominant Pied Opaline Grey Green. Big bird of good type, color, spots, and head qualities. Dark tail faulty.

Australian Banded Pied Yellowface Cobalt (Type II). Good in size, color, spots. Band runs down to flank. Patchy in color on rump.

Australian Pied Whiteflight Cobalt. Evenly marked, good color and type. Throat spots uneven.

Australian Pied Normal Cobalt. Very good size, type, color and color distribution. Band slightly small and patchy. Crouched stance due only to fright.

albinos. These difficulties, unfortunately, remain. For that purpose one can, of course, also use gray Australian pieds, as well as green pieds, for lutino production. Gray Australian pieds, even in cinnamon and opaline, can be very beautiful birds.

Most of these colors are less suited for the production of colorful "talkers" for the trade. Some dealers will not buy any grays at all, and there is only a limited demand for albinos. These birds are difficult to keep white when they are permitted to fly freely in a room.

The Violet Budgerigar

The fact that the violet budgerigar actually existed was doubted by many bird fanciers for some time. The violet factor varies widely, and in some birds it can only be recognized by experts. To most beginners, these birds look ultramarine-blue. A further confusing point are illegitimate sale offers of so-called "lilac pink" budgerigars.

The violets arose from dark blues. They are alleged to have appeared in the 1930's but subsequently disappeared. After the war, many cage-bred violets came to us from England. These were initially very expensive, rather small and not of overwhelming coloration. Yet, they were a novelty at the time and much in demand for years.

Eventually, the base colors were improved, so that even beginners could easily recognize violet budgerigars. Nowadays they are commonly displayed at shows, but despite their colors they are not that common in the pet shop trade. Why is that?

It is difficult to combine, in this bird, a satisfactory size with an excellent type and strong head. Moreover, violets invariably have throat spots which are too small. Many breeders simply do not know how to get good violet birds.

The violet factor, because it is a so-called supplementary factor, can be introduced into any other color variety. Externally (phenotypically) only one dark factor + violet factor can appear. If a large number of violet birds are to be bred, one uses the same method as described for dark blue (birds with a dark factor).

This method was discussed in detail for the green series. Essentially, it produces light green x olive-green = 100% dark progeny. Similarly, light blue (without dark factor) x mauve (two dark factors) = 100% dark blue birds. Consequently, one would expect violet light blue x violet mauve to give 100% violet (dark blue + violet factor). Unfortunately, this does not happen, since most of the violet birds have only one violet factor, and so they do not breed true. One would also expect some blues from violet pairs. Those few known homozygous violets (possessing a double factor for violet), have actually a base color which is lilac, especially in "yellow birds", which are also rather small.

Unfortunately, the show bird breeder has to make a detour in order to get birds of this color which are exhibit material.

Violet light blue and violet-mauve are essentially light blue and mauve birds with the violet factor. At first, violet light blues are difficult to distinguish from dark blues. The best distinguishing characteristics for both types are the long tail feathers: in the violet light blue they are turquoise, and in the dark blue they are pure dark blue. Violet mauve birds can be recognized on flanks and tail coverts, where the notorious spottiness in mauve birds is dark blue; but in violet-mauve birds it is often a good, clean violet. It can be transferred to progeny when mating a violet-mauve bird with a partner which does not have the violet factor (the bird without the violet factor serves to improve size). Violet light blues also have a positive influence on size, if mated with a very good dark blue bird. Such a pair can, of course, produce only a few violet offspring; the rest are light blue, violet light blue and dark blue.

As in all other representatives of the blue series, the best way to get show birds is via green. The violet factor can be

Australian Banded Pied Opaline Olive Green. Good color, markings, head and spots. Nice type. Band too large.

Australian Pied Opaline Blue (Type II). Nice, big bird of unusual color. Lacks frontal lift. Mask too small for spots.

Australian Pied Normal Dark Green. Good markings but patchy in color, lacking in body and head size. Good spots but mask too small.

Australian Pied Opaline Skyblue. Big, nicely colored bird but appears somewhat long. Head lacking in skull. Missing spots, broken band.

From lowest to highest: normal sky blue, then three green birds, one normal, one with a sex-linked cinnamon factor and the third with the gray factor. Photo by Harry V. Lacey.

transferred to the green series and it acts there as a supplementary factor, which changes colors. Then light green plus the violet factor becomes brilliant emerald-green, dark green turns to a deep but dull dark green with a silky sheen, and olive-green gets even darker. Gray-green cannot alter the violet factor, yet the gray cheek patches and the black tail feathers often have a bluish sheen in gray-green or in gray birds with violet factor.

Violet light greens, violet-gray-greens and violet-grays are the most suitable partners for improving the type and size of violets. From a cross of a violet-green bird with a violet one, which has a suitable color shade, one can expect only a few violet birds, but these will most likely satisfy all desired standard characteristics. Even among siblings of different colors, there should be some of very satisfactory coloration. The breeder has to pay particular attention that the correct size is being maintained. Therefore, only the strongest parakeets with the violet factor in green and blue should be used for breeding. The genetics of violet are not as complicated as they appear. All one has to do is to keep in mind that violet is merely a supplemental factor, which has a more or less profound influence on the base color of all varieties. It appears as violet only in dark blue birds.

Violet harlequins, Australian pieds, white wings, yellow-faced, opaline and cinnamon are also very popular—especially cinnamon birds, because of the combination with brown colors, shown in some of the better specimens as a strong pink sheen. These birds can indeed be called pink-violet, but this must not be confused with red.

Ever since budgerigars have been bred in captivity, attempts have been made to produce red birds. This is not possible, since the plumage of budgerigars does not contain any red at all. Some breeders have tried to "solve" this problem by dipping albinos into inorganic dyes. Such plumage "color" lasts, of course, only until the next molt. The Germans have tried to breed red budgerigars by inter-specific crosses with other budgerigar species which have red in their plumage. A similar method was used by canary breeders; they established red canaries with the help of the hooded finch. All these attempts failed. By the way, the so-called "pink-violet" cinnamons do not breed true, just as violets do not breed true without the cinnamon factor. Other than that, they are bred as easily as common cinnamon birds, although one must be able to accept all other colors. Moreover, the breeder should never pair cinnamon-violet x cinnamon-violet; otherwise the progeny will slowly get smaller.

Yellow-Faces and Opaline Yellow-Heads in Blue (Mutation I and II)

These color varieties became established just before the Second World War, and they were so popular that small stocks could be saved through the turmoil of the war. By then, they had fallen into some disfavor with color- and show breeders because even with birds of mutation I it was very difficult to maintain clean blue colors. With advancing age more and more yellow creeps in. Particularly, light blue yellow-faces look more turquoise than light blue from their second year on.

It is not quite as bad among dark birds, especially the gray ones. Yet, in nearly all older opaline birds (yellow-heads) there appears more and more yellow on their back, so that yellow-faced blue budgerigars (of all shades) can only be recognized as such during their first year. In addition, there is the genetic trait of yellow-faced factor I: if this is present in duplicate (homozygous) it does not appear at all externally. This strange phenomenon could not be explained for years. Eventually the hypothesis was established that the yellow-faced blue budgerigar is really a green one, with its yellow restricted to mask and tail, because the YF factor (yellow-face) suppressed the remaining yellow of the rest of the body. As a double factor, it would be fully effective and it

These young birds will soon be sold for potential show-quality,

British standard birds. Photo by Harry V. Lacey.

would then also suppress the remaining yellow. What would be left is a white-faced blue budgerigar, which is indistinguishable from the common blue one. This theory has been proven to be correct.

Thus, anyone wanting to breed yellow-faces should use such a white-faced bird and mate it with a common blue bird. The progeny from such a cross will be 100% yellow-faced. These yellow-faces possess only one YF factor and, when mated with a common blue partner, they will give rise to progeny which is partially yellow-faced and white-faced. These birds cannot inherit a YF factor.

This breeding method has the already mentioned disadvantage of causing size reduction in continuous pairing within the blue series. Anyone wanting to achieve good results at exhibitions with these color varieties has to use incrossings with the green series. The success is convincing. The disadvantage lies in the fact that "green yellow-faces" are also produced, or more precisely green birds, which suppress the yellow-face blue coloration. Such birds are totally indistinguishable from common greens. They are convenient for the breeders of yellow-faces, but others have little use for them. The reason for this is the inherent danger of introducing the YF factor into their stock from newly acquired greens. A breeder who has yellow-faces in his stock, as well as greens and common blues, cannot give any guarantees as to which greens are actual green yellow-faces and which are segregated with common blues. However, one can presume that most of the birds are segregated yellow-faced blues.

More conspicuous are the mutation II yellow-faces, both genotypically and phenotypically. Even as sub-adults they have a yellow sheen, irrespective of which shade of blue or gray they come from. Once they have obtained their adult plumage, intensively colored specimens can barely be distinguished from greens. Only dark blues and violets still show some patchiness in these colors, however, only on rump and flanks.

Mauves and grays look almost like olive-greens. Only a specialist can tell that the shading is slightly different. These can be correctly identified by picking them up and looking under their wing, where the feathers have the original base color. This is the reason why these birds, despite their beautiful golden yellow mask, have never been very popular. Since yellow-faces II are often better in type and size as show birds than yellow-faces I, these have been included in the latest revision of the standard, as a distinct color description. Still, a full class complement has rarely been achieved at a show; in fact, the same can also be said about yellow-face I. Gray yellow-faces and yellow-heads are increasing in numbers and in very good quality. Within the standard they are not in direct competition with grays but instead, like all other yellow-faces, they compete against dark birds.

COLOR COMBINATIONS

Any linking of different color factors constitutes a combination, *e.g.,* opaline blue = blue + opaline. An opaline cinnamon-blue is already a triple combination: opaline + cinnamon + blue. Here, I would like to discuss multiple combinations which create a phenotype, that is significantly different from the original pair. This method produces some very attractive intermediate forms, as well as some which are very difficult to distinguish (even by experts) as far as their genotype is concerned. The yellow-face factor (abbr. YF) has produced the most beautiful color combinations ever seen in budgerigars. The albino form of this (YF + albino) can be produced within one generation, if we start with an albino cock and a yellow-faced hen. Albino breeds sex-linked, YF is dominant, and thus all daughters are albinos and about 50% of them have yellow faces. This color combination is clearly visible in sub-adult birds. Face and tail are yellowish, the rest of the body is white. They are not particularly attractive birds; as soon as they change to their adult plumage they get a yellow tint, thus producing a lemon yellow budgerigar,

A new variety of British youngsters ready for sale.

Photo by Harry V. Lacey.

with a face mask which is of a more intense yellow than the rest of the body.

Such transitional shades become even more indistinguishable when mutation II is used. In this mutation we can breed attractive birds within a few generations as completely true, if one starts out with a pair which has an identical combination of factors (YF II + albino). In order to maintain the modern, strong form, one mates very heavy gray yellow-faces among themselves and crosses these in as soon as size and type begin to fall off.

It is equally easy to breed tri-colored pieds, with the aid of YF factors. The recessive and dominant forms of these birds are in equal demand with dealers, fanciers and breeders alike. Two generations are required for recessive pieds or harlequins. If a blue yellow-face is mated with a blue harlequin, the first generation contains white-faced- and yellow-faced blues, which are all segregated in harlequin. If these birds are mated among themselves one gets in the second generation about 13.5% yellow-faced harlequins. Their mask is yellow; all other light feather areas are white to yellowish. Blue is maintained—according to the particular shade of the original birds—on the rump, and it becomes turquoise in all remaining areas. If one includes the black markings, the progeny is really quintuplicate-colored. As in all pied birds, the overall coloration varies from one bird to the next.

Dominant pieds (Australian and Dutch) can be bred in such effective combinations within one generation. The original pairs must belong to the blue series and should consist of one pied- and one non-pied yellow-face. Color combinations and color effect of the tri- to quintuplicate-colored pied progeny are the same as in the recessive pied. However, color arrangement and markings are in accordance with the respective race. The show breeder has difficulties once again with a type of degeneration when remaining in the blue series for several generations. This problem can be eliminated through outcrossing into the green series. There are some problems here, too, because the green yellow-faced can usually not be distinguished from common greens. In addition, when using mutation I YF, the birds will have the double factor of the white-faced condition; they can only be used as breeding material when the genotype has been established through test breedings. If this is too difficult I recommend the use of mutation II yellow-face, to establish color combinations, particularly grays with a single factor.

At the beginning of the 1950's there was much publicity about the so-called rainbow colors in budgerigars. At first, breeders thought they were dealing with a new mutation. The breeding secrets were well kept, but it became apparent that this was nothing more than a combination of factors. It consists of light wings (blue white-wings, to be exact) + YF factor + opaline factor. The correct color designation would have to be white wing opaline yellow-headed dark blue or, dark violet. This same combination in light blue, mauve or even gray is too pale or too dark to deserve the name "rainbow budgerigar", although such birds are sometimes offered for sale. Despite their inferior qualities, they are still useful breeding birds.

The quickest way to produce quality rainbows is to start out—if possible—with a superior white wing light blue hen (these are, of all blue wings, the strongest) and mate it with the largest and type-correct opaline yellow-headed cock in dark blue or violet. The result is progeny with yellow-faced and white-faced normal cocks in light blue, dark blue and violet (if a violet partner was involved), as well as yellow-headed and white-headed opaline hens in the same colors. The entire progeny is segregated in white wings, and the cocks are simultaneously segregated in opaline.

If we have started with mutation I YF, we select for the second generation each a white-faced and a yellow-faced partner. For a mutation II we would use the pairing of two yellow-faced birds. In both cases, one can expect 25% white wings in dark- or light blue (or violet). Half of the offspring of mutation I are yellow-faced, and in mutation II all of them have a yellow face. Again, half will also have opaline markings; the other half will be normal. Part of the opaline birds will be yellow-headed and dark blue (or violet) at the same time, and thus we have the first true "rainbows." Mutation II will produce a few more "rainbows." However, if we compare the rainbow-colored progeny of mutation I and mutation II after the birds are in adult plumage, we will notice that the birds from mutation I have better delineated colors than those in mutation II. Most birds from mutation II remain predominantly turquoise.

The same applies to the yellow-faced white wings with normal markings (both mutations), as well as to birds in all shades of blue, all of which have dirty yellow markings. These types have to be accepted when establishing a rainbow stock.

Summarizing now, the following can be said: only yellow-headed white wing opaline violets and, at best, a good dark blue in this color factor combination, can legitimately be called a rainbow budgerigar. This budgerigar is often a delicate bird, because several factors which contribute to thin plumage and reduced size have been combined. However, this should not discourage serious breeders from trying to establish this beautiful budgerigar; after all, all the "leftover birds" can easily be disposed of also. Finally, I must caution though against offering "rainbows" which really are not true rainbows. It will always be held against the breeder who acts unethically.

BROWN WINGS

They are nothing more than opaline light wings with markings which, strangely enough, have taken on a strong brownish tone without the incrossing of cinnamons. Because of that, brown wings were considered for a long time to be a special mutant. Others believed they came about through incrossing of cinnamons. If one crosses opaline light wings, one gets offspring with greatly diluted markings and a weak base color. They look, phenotypically, like yellow and whites with a colored rump. Only opaline light wings show in their wing and back markings a brownish sheen instead of a grayish white one. These birds too are attractive and colorful, but they are definitely not a mutation, as has often been maintained. Without the YF factor brown wings are not difficult to breed. One really only needs well-marked opalines, preferably royal opaline with reduced black markings, to breed with light wings (see: Green Yellow-Wings and Blue White-Wings): 1,0 opaline × 0,1 light wing = normal cocks (segregated in opaline and light wing), opaline hens (segregated in light wing). The following generation produces 25% light wings of both sexes and half of these in opaline. The most beautiful specimens have bright blue plumage, with markings restricted to the wings. The primary feathers have a grayish brown tone (primary light feathers and tail feathers = brown wing). The British call these birds "selves" (uniformly colored), and they have established special show classes for them.

CINNAMON GRAYWINGS

I have to caution breeders against random linking of other factors promoting a color reduction. The cinnamon graywings are a good example of this. These birds are occasionally seen in a generally good type, but with totally unrecognizable markings, as well as with a pale base color. The same holds true for pieds in graywing, light wing, yellow or white with green or blue (respectively) rump, lacewings in fallow, cinnamon fallow, light graywings, etc. It is, of course, up to the individual to make controlled experiments in any direction. However, the majority of breeders hold the opinion that the "fall out birds" from such experiments should not be displayed at shows.

SLATE

This gray-blue, sex-linked mutation, has a base color which is somewhere between mauve and gray. So far, it has been restricted to the British Isles, and it is becoming rare over there too. The slate factor changes (darkens) blue and green equally, and it can be bred in three shades; light, medium, dark. Theoretically, it is transmittable to all color varieties; however, the results are not supposed to be overwhelming.

CRESTED

Crested budgerigars appeared in the 1950's, first in Canada, and in the 1960's in Europe. The heredity of crests is dominant, as it is in all domesticated birds with crests. However, according to ZISWILER there is a 46% lethal factor involved, which appears to be the reason why few crested birds reach adulthood. The standard distinguishes between pointed, half- and complete crests, whereby the birds with pointed crests are the most common and fittest ones. Crests can be bred in all colors, but they are inclined towards size reduction.

HALF-SIDERS

They are a curiosity of nature. Half-siders belong neither to the green series nor to the blue series: they are green on one side and blue on the other. Some specimens have a completely symmetrical dividing line across the middle of the body; in others it may be diagonal, in other words, asymmetrical.

In a show cage, the arrangement of perches permits viewing of only one side of such a bird. This has fooled even judges. One thinks, for instance, one is looking at a green budgerigar, which appears to be the same as any other bird of this kind. Then, unnoticed, the bird turns around and suddenly the same bird is blue. Cage numbers are being compared, everything seems to be okay, but the bird looks different!!

The colors of most half-siders are evenly shaded, *e.g.,* light green and light blue, dark green and dark blue, etc. There are also half-siders in dark green and light blue and in other shades. Half-siders can occur in all known color varieties. The most conspicuous half-sider I have ever seen was a quintuplicate-colored harlequin in dark green and dark blue, with partially yellow and white patches and black markings.

Half-siders are not a mutation and so they do not breed true. At best, one refers to this phenomenon as a genetic tendency towards the formation of half-siders in certain stocks. Most of them are, genotypically, green segregated in blue. They are predominantly small birds of a poor type. Half-siders are always popular at shows. They add a touch of novelty, and so they often receive a special prize in the AOC (any other color) class.

REFERENCES

AICHELE, D., Dr.: Das bluht an allen Wegen. Stuttgart (1971).

AICHELE, D., Dr.: Was bluht denn da? Stuttgart (1973).

ARMOUR, M.D.S., Dr.: Exhibition Budgerigars. London (year not indicated).

AZ-DKB-Einheitsstandard. Herne. (1976).

BENL, G.: Vererbung. Eine kurze Grundlage der allgemeinen Genetik. Minden (1969).

DUNCKER, H., Dr.: Vererbungslehre fur Kleinvogelzuchter. Leipzig (1929).

ELIOTT, F.S., and E.W. BROOKS: Budgerigar Matings and Colour Expectations. Derby (1953).

ENEHJELM, C. AF: Das Buch vom Wellensittich. Pfungstadt/Darmstadt (1957).

ENEHJELM, C. AF: Kafige und Volieren. Stuttgart (1969).

IMMELMANN, K., Prof. Dr.: Im unbekannten Australien. Pfungstadt/Darmstadt (1960).

IMMELMANN, K., Prof. Dr.: Die australischen Plattschweifsittiche. Wittenberg (1964).

KEMNA, A., Dr.: Krankheiten der Stubenvogel. Minden (year not indicated).

KOLAR, S., und G.A. RADTKE: Farbiger Fehlerfinder fur Wellensittiche. Braunschweig (2nd Edition 1976).

KRONBERGER, H., Dr.: Haltung von Vogeln - Krankheiten der Vogel. Jena (1974).

MARSDEN, PH.: Das Wellensittich-A-B-C. Zurich und Stuttgart (1966).

NICOLAI, J., Dr.: Vogelhaltung - Vogelpflege. Stuttgart (1965).

RADTKE, G.A.: Wellensittiche - mein Hobby. Stuttgart (6th Edition 1978).

RADTKE, G.A.: Farbiger Rassenatlas fur Wellensittiche. Braunschweig.

RADTKE, G.A.: Die Farbschlage des Wellensittichs. Minden (9th Edition 1978).

RADTKE, G.A.: Farbenkanarien. Minden (5th Edition (1976).

RADTKE, G.A.: Positurkanarien und Mischlinge. Minden (2nd Edition 1976).

RAETHEL, S.: Krankheiten der Stubenvogel. Stuttgart (1966).

RAGOTZI, B.: Freude am Wellensittich. Berlin (1959).

REINHARDT, F.: Kobold Tschirri, der sprechende Wellensittich. Stuttgart (1964).

ROGERS, C.: Parakeet Guide. New York (1970).

RUTGERS, A.: Wellensittiche pfleglich gehalten und kundig gezuchtet. Stuttgart (1972).

SABEL, K.: Vogelfutterpflanzen. Pfungstadt (1967).

STEINER, H., Prof. Dr.: Vererbungsstudien am Wellensittich. Zurich (1932).

SWIFT, G.S.K.: Vom Wellensittich Fabian. Zurich und Stuttgart (1965).

TAYLOR, T.G., Dr., und C. WARNER: Genetics for Budgerigar Breeders. London (1961).

TAYLOR, T.G., Dr.: Feeding Exhibition Budgerigars. London (1958).

ZISWILER, V., Prof. Dr.: Erbgang und Manifestationsmuster des Faktors, "Haube", eines Subvitalfaktors des Wellensittichs, Melopsittacus undulatus. Archiv der Julius-Klaus-Stiftung fur Vererbungsforschung, Sozialanthropologie und Rassenhygiene. 38(1963), p. 145-165.

INDEX